Pedometer Power

Using Pedometers in School and Community

SECOND EDITION

Pedometer Power

Using Pedometers in School and Community
SECOND EDITION

Robert P. Pangrazi
Aaron Beighle
Cara L. Sidman

Human Kinetics

Library of Congress Cataloging-in-Publication Data

Pangrazi, Robert P.
  Pedometer power : using pedometers in school and community / Robert P. Pangrazi, Aaron Beighle, Cara L. Sidman. -- 2nd ed.
     p. cm.
  Includes bibliographical references.
  ISBN-13: 978-0-7360-6272-5 (soft cover)
  ISBN-10: 0-7360-6272-6 (soft cover)
  1. Exercise--Measurement. 2. Physical education and training. I. Beighle, Aaron, 1972-
II. Sidman, Cara L., 1972-   III. Title.
  QP301.P34   2007
  612' .044--dc22

                                                       2007001888

ISBN-10: 0-7360-6272-6
ISBN-13: 978-0-7360-6272-5

The Web addresses cited in this text were current as of March 8, 2007, unless otherwise noted.

Acquisitions Editor: Bonnie Pettifor Vreeland; **Managing Editor:** Bethany J. Bentley; **Copyeditor:** Annette Pierce; **Proofreader:** Erin Cler; **Permission Manager:** Dalene Reeder; **Graphic Designer:** Nancy Rasmus; **Graphic Artist:** Francine Hamerski; **Photo Asset Manager:** Laura Fitch; **Cover Designer:** Keith Blomberg; **Photographer (interior and cover):** Neil Bernstein, unless otherwise noted; **Art Manager:** Kelly Hendren; **Illustrator:** Al Wilborn; **Printer:** Versa Press

We thank the YMCA in Champaign, Illinois, for assistance in providing the location for the photo shoot for page 37 of this book.

Printed in the United States of America   10 9 8 7 6 5 4 3 2 1

Human Kinetics
Web site: www.HumanKinetics.com

United States: Human Kinetics
P.O. Box 5076
Champaign, IL 61825-5076
800-747-4457
e-mail: humank@hkusa.com

Canada: Human Kinetics
475 Devonshire Road Unit 100
Windsor, ON N8Y 2L5
800-465-7301 (in Canada only)
e-mail: orders@hkcanada.com

Europe: Human Kinetics
107 Bradford Road
Stanningley
Leeds LS28 6AT, United Kingdom
+44 (0) 113 255 5665
e-mail: hk@hkeurope.com

Australia: Human Kinetics
57A Price Avenue
Lower Mitcham, South Australia 5062
08 8372 0999
e-mail: liaw@hkaustralia.com

New Zealand: Human Kinetics
Division of Sports Distributors NZ Ltd.
P.O. Box 300 226 Albany
North Shore City
Auckland
0064 9 448 1207
e-mail: info@humankinetics.co.nz

Contents

7 Activities for Families and Communities   145

Preface

The first edition of *Pedometer Power* was written at a time when pedometers were just beginning to be used in schools, health clubs, and other health care settings. We thought that pedometers could be a valuable tool in promoting active and healthy lifestyles, but there was little supportive evidence available. This second edition is much improved because the activities and ideas are supported by actual programs and research data. The pedometer has become an accepted tool for objectively measuring physical activity in a variety of settings. Evidence points to a rapid increase in obesity in many countries, and lack of physical activity is a root cause. Studies also show that people tend to overestimate the amount of daily physical activity they accumulate. Now daily activity can be quantified with accurate and sophisticated pedometers. Pedometers can indicate the time of day the physical activity was done, measure the intensity of activity, store many days' worth of data on physical activity, and record the length of bouts of activity. Just as pedometer technology continues to improve, we have worked diligently to offer more information and instructional ideas to a varied audience.

The look and feel of this edition have changed dramatically from our first effort. Chapter 1 offers a clear discussion about pedometers and research evidence that supports their effectiveness in monitoring physical activity. For years, it was believed that the only activity that "counted" had to be intense and demanding. This chapter explains how moderate to vigorous activity can offer ample health benefits, making it much more palatable to the masses. The question of how much activity is adequate for good health is often asked, and we have made an effort to answer it by showing that pedometers can monitor the nationally recommended guidelines. The focus of the chapter is to show that a different paradigm of activity habits is easy to monitor with pedometers and also appeals more to the masses.

Chapter 2 is a nuts-and-bolts chapter designed to help teachers and health professionals deal with frequently asked questions. Basic questions (How do I find money to buy pedometers? How much should I pay? Do I get what I pay for? What is the best way to manage my pedometers?) are answered in detail. Practical ideas and applications are presented, which are based on our experience and the experiences of fellow professionals.

Chapter 3 covers the use of pedometers in physical education settings. One of the most difficult aspects of using pedometers in schools is making it easy for students and teachers to use them without disrupting the class. If pedometers cause physical educators too many problems, it is likely they will stop using the devices in their classes. Routines for students are offered so that getting a pedometer, resetting it, and checking it at the end of the period are habits that students perform without being told. Pedometers offer teachers valuable feedback about the amount of activity students get in classes as well as outside the physical education setting. Chapters 2 and 3 will equip you with the knowledge you need to use pedometers successfully.

Getting people to move independently is a goal for all professionals in the physical activity field. Chapter 4 is a new chapter designed to get people to manage their own activity programs. Motivation, self-efficacy, and goal setting are woven together in the chapter to help students and adults learn to monitor and design personal activity strategies. Setting goals for discretionary-time activity and learning how to convert steps to miles and kilometers are included in this chapter.

Chapter 5 is an accumulation of many instructional activities for elementary physical education teachers. Students learn how to use a pedometer that can measure both activity time and steps. Estimating distance and time is taught through walking activities. Orienteering skills, understanding differences in stride length between individuals, and graphing activity data are some of the academic integration skills presented in chapter 5. In addition, there are many activities for physical education classes and ideas for schoolwide events. This chapter shows how to integrate pedometers into an already-solid physical education program.

The previous edition contained only a few activities and ideas for secondary school and college students. Chapter 6 is expanded to include many new activities that are educational and developmentally appropriate. The worksheets can be used for a college-level introductory course on pedometers. Coauthor Cara Sidman field-tested the activities in chapter 6 and found them to be both practical and motivating for high school and college students.

As pedometers become more common in the school curriculum, physical education teachers and classroom teachers can generate ideas on ways to integrate pedometers and self-management skills into the classroom with minimal disruption. Many ideas for integrating pedometer data into other academic areas are presented in chapters 4, 5, and 6. All of those ideas are marked with this symbol: 📚.

To bring the book full circle, activities for families and communities are expanded in chapter 7. The use of pedometers is limited if they don't have an effect on youth outside of their educational circle. In addition, if parents and children can learn the basics of choosing physical activities that contribute to the health of everyone, then everyone benefits. The activities in this chapter stir some friendly competition among family members and help children and parents learn about the community. Finally, schools and community organizations can work together to find ways to make the community a more active place.

We hope that you view *Pedometer Power* as a starting point for your creativity. And we hope this text will help you adapt ideas to meet your needs, create new activities, and help others develop active lifestyles. That is the spirit we want to share with you. May all your physical activity be a positive experience, and may your health benefit through your efforts.

Promoting Lifestyle Physical Activity

For more than 40 years, children have been viewed as being unfit, a problem that could be rectified with strenuous and structured physical activity. The goal was to push youth to develop high levels of physical fitness without concern for long-term impact. An underlying assumption was that if we "got them fit" as youth, certainly they would stay fit as adults. Obviously, this assumption was incorrect, and today we are in the middle of a battle with the bulge. In the '90s, research analyzing previous United States national data (Corbin & Pangrazi, 1992) showed that the fitness levels of youth had not decreased and, in fact, had even increased in some cases (with the exception of obesity). Also, evidence demonstrating the influence of variables such as genetics, maturation, and trainability (all of which children have no control over) on physical fitness test performance began to mount (Corbin & Pangrazi, 1992). This brought about a shift in thinking. If fitness testing discouraged many of the youth who had done poorly or failed the fitness test and children had little control over the variables that affected their performance the most, what was the point? If pushing youth to be fit often backfired when the kids who needed it the most hated it the most, something needed to change.

From Fitness to Physical Activity

A new approach grew out of this shift in thinking: one that placed strong emphasis on promoting physical activity for all youth regardless of ability level and other genetic limitations. This shift from structured and often forced exercises to lifestyle physical activity is supported by scientific studies that have demonstrated benefits from moderate amounts of activity (Dunn, Andersen, & Jakicic, 1998). This emerging philosophy focuses on the process of performing daily physical activity, not the outcome of obtaining a high score on physical fitness test batteries. Such an approach is also supported by Healthy People 2010, national goals for America, which has a primary objective to "improve health, fitness, and quality of life through daily physical activity" (USDHHS, 1998, p. 22). Fitness and lifestyle activity are related because continued participation in physically active lifestyles may ultimately lead to physical fitness. However, many factors, such as those described earlier, influence the extent to which an individual is capable of attaining physical fitness; whereas, every child can successfully reach physical activity goals, a behavior within reach of all individuals.

Benefits of Physical Activity

With the focus in physical education shifting toward physical activity and away from fitness, it is important to establish the link between physical activity and health benefits. This link also provides the rationale for physical educators to promote and implement the pedometer programs and ideas outlined in this book. Two key studies that prompted national health concern about sedentary living were based on epidemiological findings relating physical activity to a reduction in mortality rates in men. Paffenbarger and his colleagues (Paffenbarger, Hyde, Wing, & Hsieh, 1986) examined more than 16,000 Harvard alumni over a span of 12 to 16 years and identified a positive relationship between physical activity and longevity, and reduction in mortality from all causes. Their results illustrated a clear 10 percent advantage for men expending more than 2,000 calories (8,400 kilojoules) per week, with some benefits seen at weekly caloric expenditures of 500 calories (2,100 kilojoules). This dose–response relationship (how much activity is necessary to cause positive health changes) has consequently become the focus of further investigation with regard to both physical and psychological benefits.

Blair and his colleagues also conducted noteworthy research alerting the public of the important benefits of regular physical activity and fitness (Blair et al., 1995; Blair & Brodney, 1999). In one study, they examined approximately 10,000 healthy and unhealthy men over five years to determine the relationship between physical fitness changes and risk of mortality. Their results indicated that physical fitness could reduce all-cause mortality and cardiovascular disease. In another study, Blair and Brodney (1999) analyzed more than 700 studies that met specific inclusion criteria to determine if participation in physical activity as well as actually attaining physical fitness reduce the risk of morbidity and mortality and other health-related outcome measures. Based on these prospective observational studies, they determined that physical activity does indeed attenuate the health risks associated with obesity. In addition, they found that a person who is of normal weight, but sedentary, is at a greater health risk than an overweight or obese physically active person. Essentially, the results from these studies indicated that inactivity and cardiovascular fitness are just as important in predicting morbidity and mortality as overweight and obesity. Although most of the pioneering epidemiological studies were based on adult men, the benefit of physical activity and fitness to health has been well established for all individuals.

There are benefits from daily physical activity that affect healthy growth and development for youth. This claim is supported by numerous studies that provide convincing evidence that decreased physical activity puts children at risk for a variety of diseases. Not surprising, many of these diseases are associated with being overweight and inactive (USDHHS, 1996). Specifically, being overweight during childhood is related to an increased risk for diseases such as noninsulin-dependent diabetes mellitus (NIDDM), hypercholesterolemia, hypertension, and orthopedic problems, all of which are traditionally thought of as "adult" medical problems (Bar-Or et al., 1998). Another aspect of children's health affected by physical activity is bone density. In fact, physical activity participation at an early age improves peak bone density during critical growth periods (Sallis & McKenzie, 1991). In a study by Bailey and colleagues (1995), bouts of intermittent physical activity (alternating periods of vigorous activity and rest) stimulated the release of the growth hormone. This pattern of activity is typical of youth and appears to be necessary to assure optimal growth. Overweight and physical inactivity behaviors track from childhood to adulthood (Whitaker et al., 1997; Malina, 1996). Thus, youth who are inactive or overweight are more likely to become inactive or overweight adults. This results in a compounding effect with inactive children having the potential to become overweight children who become inactive, overweight adults.

Investigators continue to study the relationship between the amount of activity and the subsequent benefits. This is knowledge that health and physical educators need when they teach and when they recommend daily activity for their students. It also has an effect on the design of high-quality physical education programs because adequate opportunity must be built into the curriculum to positively affect the health of youth (Haskell, 1994).

From Intensity to Volume

With the benefits of physical activity clearly established, the past decade has brought to the forefront research on the type of physical activity best prescribed for favorable health, fitness, and performance outcomes. Because of the escalating problem of obesity and its associated health risks in youth today, the focus of this book is on ways to promote and facilitate physical activity leading to health benefits. Evidence exists that virtually anyone can benefit from daily moderate to vigorous physical activity (Haskell, 1994). However, it is difficult to quantify moderate to vigorous activity (often characterized as a brisk walk), and many people are turned off by the focus on intense physical activity. Fortunately, there is an alternative that is easier to measure and more acceptable: monitoring the volume of activity (duration and frequency) rather than the intensity of activity to reach health goals. Essentially, the dose–response relationship, according to Haskell (1994), refers to the premise that as the amount of activity increases, benefits increase.

Research by Dunn and colleagues (1999) sought to investigate the specific type of physical activity needed to elicit health benefits. These researchers conducted a study to determine the effects of lifestyle activity and structured activity on subsequent physical activity level and cardiorespiratory fitness. Lifestyle activity was defined as 30 minutes or more of accumulated moderate-intensity physical activity that was part of daily routines on most or all days of the week as described in the U.S. Surgeon General's guidelines (USDHHS, 1996). Structured activity involved a traditional exercise prescription, requiring an intensity of 50 to 85 percent of maximal aerobic power for 20 to 60 minutes and attending at least three supervised workout sessions a week. After 24 months, physical activity was measured by a seven-day recall questionnaire, and cardiorespiratory fitness was measured by a maximal treadmill test. Cholesterol, blood pressure, and body composition were also included as secondary outcomes.

Dunn and colleagues (1999) concluded that lifestyle activity intervention was as effective as structured activity intervention in improving physical activity and fitness levels among previously sedentary healthy adults. Therefore, the traditional structured-exercise prescription recommending 20 to 60 minutes of physical activity at a specific intensity level is modifiable, depending on goals. For physical educators, if the goal is to teach students the benefits of physical activity and ultimately turn them on to a lifetime of activity participation, using lifestyle intervention (as the U.S. Surgeon General recommends) is sufficient and probably more effective than structured intervention in developing and maintaining positive attitudes.

Because a number of studies have shown such positive findings, researchers are focusing on the total amount (volume) of physical activity performed daily rather than on high-intensity physical activity. Health and physical educators need to be armed with this knowledge when they teach and recommend daily activities for their students. They can use it to design high-quality physical education programs that positively affect the health of students (Haskell, 1994). Instructors who develop and revise physical education curriculums should consider the U.S. Surgeon General's lifetime activity guidelines and the unique physical activity needs of students (Pangrazi, Corbin, & Welk, 1996).

Pedometers offer an easy and effective way to monitor the volume of accumulated physical activity in terms of step counts among various populations. A cross-sectional analysis of a predominantly female (86.8 percent) participant population approaching the criterion for obesity found an inverse relationship between the number of steps per day and various health indicators such as body mass index (BMI), waist circumference, and diastolic blood pressure (Chan, Spangler, Valcour, & Tudor-Locke, 2003). Additional support for this relationship between pedometer-determined volume of activity and health outcomes has been reported in more-healthy adult populations including African American middle-aged women (Hornbuckle, Bassett, & Thompson, 2005; Thompson, Rakow, & Perdue, 2004). These findings have strong implications for public health and quality of life. Because cardiovascular disease is highly preventable through healthier lifestyle choices (Corbin, Welk,

Corbin, & Welk, 2008), educational programs can play an integral role in the improvement of the health of the population. Specifically, increasing physical activity participation in the schools and promoting lifetime physical activity at a young age can help countries reach their fitness goals by the year 2010.

How Much Physical Activity Is Enough?

Multiple recommendations for physical activity exist, which often makes it difficult to know the minimal amount of activity required for individuals with different needs. The answer to this question depends on the goals sought and the population involved. For example, the amount of physical activity that is necessary for good health is less than the amount necessary for high levels of athletic fitness. In addition, children require greater amounts of physical activity than adults.

Current Youth Physical Activity Levels

With increased awareness of the importance of physical activity for children, the amount of research examining the physical activity levels of youth has increased. Recently, researchers have been using pedometers to assess the physical activity levels of children. This is of particular importance because pedometers are becoming popular tools for assessing physical activity in physical education as well. With researchers and physical educators using the same tools, the transfer of knowledge from research to application and vice versa is much easier.

But just how active are children and what are these studies finding? One study used pedometers to measure the physical activity levels of children in Australia, Sweden, and the United States (Vincent, Pangrazi, Raustorp, Tomson, & Cuddihy, 2003). A total of 1,954 6- to 12-year-olds wore pedometers for four consecutive weekdays. Figure 1.1 illustrates the physical activity levels of boys and girls in each country. Australian and Swedish children were uniformly more active than children from the United States. The authors of this study cite the physical structure of the community and the structure of the school day as potential factors that may influence physical activity. Interestingly, during the school day in the United States, children were given 410 minutes of activity time (recess and physical education) per week, whereas in Sweden, students were allowed 580 minutes of activity time per week. Divided out over a five-day school week, Swedish children were given almost 34 more minutes of activity time per week. To further support the claim that European children are more active than American children, a study of

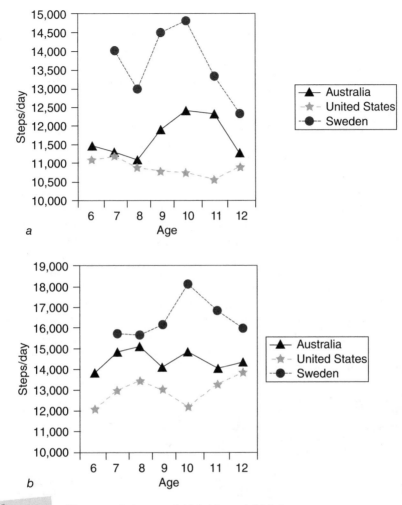

a

b

Figure 1.1   Step counts by age *(a)* in girls and *(b)* in boys.

Adapted, by permission, from S.D. Vincent, R.P. Pangrazi, A. Raustorp, L.M. Tomson, and T.F. Cuddihy, 2003, "Activity levels and body mass index of children in the United States, Sweden, and Australia," *Medicine and Science in Sports and Exercise* 35(8): 1367-1373.

children from North Wales found that boys accumulated 16,035 steps per day and girls 12,728 steps per day (Rowlands and Eston, 2005). These numbers are comparable to the steps per day data of the Swedish children and greater than the physical activity level of the U.S. children.

Discussion is in order here regarding the activity differences between boys and girls. Most research examining the physical activity levels of children shows boys to be more active than girls in all countries.

However, this difference may be due to maturity rather than inherent differences in the drive to be active. A study (Thompson, Baxter-Jones, Mirwald, & Bailey, 2003) showed that there was a difference in activity levels when children were classified by age. However, when the same children were classified by biological age, there were no differences in activity level except three years before peak height velocity (growth spurt). Because girls are usually one to two years more mature than boys at the same age, this may explain some of the activity difference in activity levels when students are classified by chronological age.

Another study using American children examined the physical activity levels of 1,839 students in grades 1 through 12. The primary finding from this study indicated that physical activity level does decrease with age; however, it may not occur as early as previously thought, particularly when physical activity is assessed using pedometers. As figure 1.2 shows, around the sixth or seventh grade (11 or 12 years of age), the number of steps accumulated daily begins to decline. One potential cause of this decline could be student access to physical activity opportunities. In middle schools, activity opportunities such as recess, physical education, after-school programs, and sports participation are either eliminated or decreased. Although much more research in this area is necessary, this study suggests that the school environment may contribute to the decline in physical activity as students move from elementary schools to secondary schools.

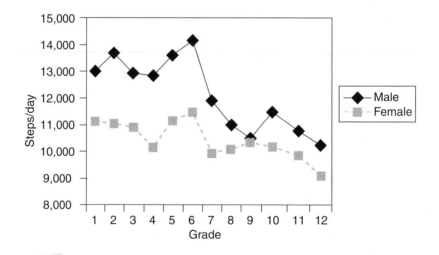

Figure 1.2   Average steps per day for boys and girls, grades 1 through 12.

Adapted, by permission, from G. Le Masurier et al., 2005, "Pedometer-determined physical activity levels of youth," *Journal of Physical Activity and Health* 2(2): 159-168.

Activity Patterns of Youth

Although understanding the daily physical activity levels of children is important, it is also important to understand when and where children are physically active. That is, during what parts of the day are students active? One study divided the day into three parts: physical education, the remainder of the school day, and outside of school (Morgan, Pangrazi, & Beighle, 2003). Figure 1.3 is a graphic representation of the results. These data suggest that children receive meaningful amounts of physical activity during all three periods of the day. Tudor-Locke and colleagues (2006) used American sixth graders to provide a more detailed description of physical activity throughout the day. The day was divided into before school, lunchtime recess, physical education, and after school. These students were most active after school, followed by lunchtime recess, before school, and during physical education. Because most of their day was spent outside of school, a majority of their physical activity was accumulated during that time; however, the school day offers an excellent opportunity for students to accumulate physical activity.

Although not often looked at as a source of physical activity, schools hold much potential for providing students with useful physical activity opportunities. One of the sources is physical education. It is important to understand that the physical activity level of students depends on many

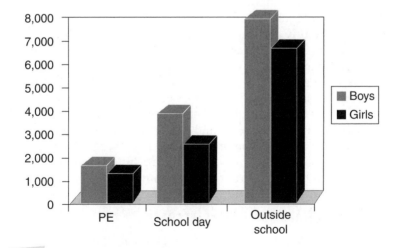

Figure 1.3   Step counts of students during physical education, the school day, and outside of school.

Adapted from C.F. Morgan, R.P. Pangrazi, and A. Beighle, 2003, "Using pedometers to promote physical activity in physical education," *Journal of Physical Education, Recreation and Dance* 74(7): 33-38.

factors, including the type of lesson, quality of lesson, and instructional time. Very few studies have looked at the physical activity levels of U.S. students during physical education. For girls the step counts range from 1,300 to 1,800 and for boys 1,400 to 1,900 in a 30-minute physical education lesson (Scruggs et al., 2003; Morgan, Pangrazi, & Beighle, 2003; Tudor-Locke et al., 2006). These numbers are not presented to establish a goal for physical educators, but rather to provide a starting point for discussion. Again, each school, physical education program, and class will be different. For this reason, the most effective approach is to establish baseline data and determine physical education step goals based on those data. See chapter 4 for more details on goal setting and chapter 3 for information on recording pedometer data in physical education.

Another source of physical activity is during activity breaks, or recess. Research on the activity levels of children during recess is limited, especially research using pedometers. One study measured the number of steps and the amount of time U.S. students were active during a 15-minute recess over four consecutive days (Beighle and Pangrazi, 2006). Boys accumulated 1,268 steps and girls 914 steps in just 15 minutes. Stated another way, boys spent 78 percent of the recess time (11.7 minutes) and girls spent 63 percent of their recess time (9.4 minutes) engaged in physical activity. These data suggest that recess, in a short amount of time, offers meaningful amounts of physical activity. This same study also looked at physical activity outside of school. The authors refer to these two times, outside of school and recess, as discretionary time in which students have some choice in their physical activity behaviors. Boys and girls in this study accumulated 7,229 and 5,808 steps, respectively, outside of school. Other studies have found that physical activity outside of school accounted for nearly half of the total number of steps children accumulate throughout the day (Tudor-Locke et al., 2006; Morgan, Pangrazi, & Beighle, 2003). Research using pedometers to assess the physical activity levels of children reveals that steps are accumulated during both the school day during recess and physical education and outside of the school day. For this reason, interventions and programs designed to increase the physical activity levels of children must be comprehensive and involve both the schools and the community.

Activity Guidelines for Preadolescents

The National Association for Sport and Physical Education (NASPE) activity guidelines for elementary school children in the United States (2004) call for 60 minutes or more of physical activity (total volume) for children and youth. Two of the four major activity guidelines are briefly described as follows. For in-depth information about all of the physical activity guidelines for children, see the NASPE document (2004).

Guideline 1

Children should accumulate at least 60 minutes and up to several hours of age-appropriate physical activity on all or most days of the week. This daily accumulation should include moderate and vigorous physical activity with the majority being intermittent in nature.

Sixty minutes is the minimum amount of daily activity recommended for children. It is becoming increasingly clear that 60 minutes is a minimal level of activity; much more is needed. For example, using data collected with a pedometer that measures activity time and steps, 60 minutes of physical activity equated to slightly more than 5,000 steps. In the United States, the President's Council on Physical Fitness and Sports (2006) has established the Presidential Active Lifestyle Award threshold of 11,000 and 13,000 steps for girls and boys, respectively. This makes it obvious that 60 minutes is the minimum amount youth should accumulate on a daily basis. Physical activity minutes accumulated each day should include some moderate activity equal in intensity to brisk walking and some vigorous activity of greater intensity than brisk walking. For children, most activity will come in intermittent activity bursts ranging from a few seconds to several minutes alternating with rest periods. Continuous vigorous physical activity of several minutes should not be expected for most children, nor should it be a condition for meeting the guidelines.

Guideline 2

Children should participate in several bouts of physical activity lasting 15 minutes or more each day.

Much of a child's daily activity will be in short bursts and accumulated throughout the day. However, if optimal benefits are to accrue, much of the activity should be accumulated in bouts of 15 minutes or more. Examples of physical activity bouts are recess, physical education, play periods, and sports practices. This guideline illustrates the importance of a 15-minute recess in the health and development of children. It is indefensible to eliminate recess and time for physical activity, a trend all too common in today's schools. To be clear, these bouts of 15 minutes or more are not expected to include continuous activity such as jogging on a track. Instead, they will include physical activity and opportunity for social development.

Activity Guidelines for Adolescents

A consensus statement that recommends the amount of activity adolescents should perform regularly has been developed by a board of experts (Strong et al., 2005). This statement delineates the amount of activity adolescents (ages 11 to 21) need and contains two basic guidelines. Guideline 1 states that "all adolescents should be physically active daily, or nearly

© Human Kinetics

Adolescents should do some form of physical activity
nearly every day.

every day, as part of play, games, sports, work, transportation, recreation, physical education, or planned exercise, in the context of family, school, and community activities" (Sallis & Patrick, 1994). Adolescents who participate in the 30 minutes of activity discussed earlier in this chapter meet the first guideline. Guideline 2 states that "adolescents should engage in 3 or more sessions per week of activities that last 20 minutes or more and require moderate to vigorous levels of exertion" (Sallis & Patrick, 1994).

Meeting guideline 1 should be a priority and the minimum goal. Participation in 30 minutes of daily activity is a reasonable goal, even for sedentary youth. Beyond this, guideline 2 is a desirable goal. The consensus statement includes brisk walking, jogging, stair climbing, basketball, racket sports, soccer, dance, lap swimming, skating, strength (resistance) training, lawn mowing, and cycling as examples of activities that meet guideline 2. Maintaining the heart rate at a preselected target heart rate for the full 20 minutes is not necessary to meet guideline 2, and many of the activities listed do not produce such a result.

Step and Activity Time Cut Points

One set of recommendations that can be measured via pedometry are requirements, or cut points, that elementary students must achieve in order to earn the Presidential Active Lifestyle Award (President's Council on Physical Fitness and Sports, 2006). Based on data using more than 600 elementary-age students in the United States, award cut points were set at 11,000 daily step counts (DSC) for girls and 13,000 DSC for boys. It is important to note that these recommendations do not suggest that students should use this single cut point as their goal. In fact, another component of this award is a goal-setting option that offers the opportunity to customize activity requirements to the unique needs of each student. The benefits of when and how to use goal setting will be discussed in a later chapter.

When most people ask "How much physical activity is enough?" what they are really asking is "How much physical activity is enough to produce health benefits?" The guidelines stated earlier are norm referenced and are not linked to health outcomes. Very little evidence is available to suggest that children who reach these guidelines are any healthier than children who do not. In 2005, a panel of experts convened and identified 850 studies and review articles examining the effects of physical activity on health (Strong et al., 2005). After extensive review, the panel recommended that school-aged youth engage in 60 or more minutes of moderate to vigorous physical activity that is developmentally appropriate and enjoyable. This recommendation was based on intervention data and reasonable expectations regarding the amount of time children have available to be active in a typical day.

Another group of researchers (Tudor-Locke et al., 2004) developed BMI-referenced standards for steps per day for children. Using nearly 2,000 children in grades one through six from Australia, Sweden, and the United States, overweight cut points of 12,000 steps per day for girls and 15,000 steps per day for boys were established. Children who met or exceeded these daily step counts were more likely to be classified as being of normal weight as indicated by international cut points. It must be noted that the cut points in this study may be high for American children because the data bank included Swedish and Australian children who were more active. This preliminary study is the first to link steps per day with a known health indicator.

Physical activity guidelines in units of steps and minutes can be confusing. An often-asked question is, "If I take this many steps, how many minutes is it?" A recent study developed an equation to help answer this question. Using a pedometer that assesses both steps and activity time, Beighle and Pangrazi (2006) established a preliminary equation: minutes of activity = $0.01 \times$ total daily steps + 14.5. This converts steps to minutes and minutes to steps. Using this equation, 10,000 steps equal 114.5 minutes of activity. However, keep in mind several points when using this equation. First, it is the first equation of its kind and thus much more research is necessary before drawing conclusions about its reliability. Also, the equation is based on daily free-living activity. The equation for structured activity, such as physical education, is likely to be different. Lastly, this equation does not allow conclusions to be made about the intensity of activity. In spite of these limitations, this equation has potential for use by practitioners wishing to convert step counts to total amount of time spent stepping. In a study that examines the relationship between 60-plus minutes of moderate to vigorous physical activity and the BMI-referenced standards, Rowlands and Eston (2005) used accelerometers and pedometers on 8- to 10-year-old children. The authors concluded that boys who accumulated 13,000 steps per day and girls who accumulated 12,000 steps per day engaged in sufficient amounts of physical activity to meet the 60-plus-minute standard.

Active and Healthy School Programs

Physical educators play an important role in teaching children ways to meet physical activity guidelines, and the manner in which they do so is crucial. They teach a variety of children, all different, and with widely varying physical capacities. This implies taking into account different skill and fitness levels and how these differences are affected and influenced by heredity. The role of heredity in determining physical fitness abilities is well documented (Bouchard, 1999). For example, only a small percentage of children have the genetic predisposition to be able to perform the optimal number of pull-ups to place them in the high fitness zone on youth fitness tests. However, all children can be physically active when walking or performing other locomotor movements. Because high-level fitness performance is impossible for the vast majority of youth, it becomes important to place the majority of emphasis on lifestyle physical activity. All students, regardless of their physical limitations, can perform lifestyle activity. Successful lifestyle experiences in a "can do" environment increase the chance that youth will meet physical activity guidelines as well as mature into active adults.

In spite of this new information and knowledge, some physical education programs continue to promote physical fitness outcomes rather than make the shift toward promoting lifestyle physical activity. Physical fitness tests remain the most common form of evaluation in physical education (Hopple & Graham, 1995). Beighle, Pangrazi, and Vincent (2001) recently proposed that evaluation of youth should focus on identifying children who are physically inactive. The focus on fitness goals does little to help identify youth who are inactive. When genetically blessed children can achieve high fitness scores without accumulating adequate amounts of daily physical activity, chances are that they may leave school believing fitness can be achieved without being active. Similarly, youth who are physically active and spend a lot of time training may still score poorly on a fitness test because of their genetic limitations. This creates a disappointing scenario that can lead to a "what's the use of trying" attitude because of their lack of improvement on fitness tests. Essentially, the role of fitness testing for accountability in physical education needs to be reviewed. It is one thing to teach youth how to personally evaluate their own fitness levels as they participate in self-testing activities. However, to use fitness testing for grading or to evaluate the success of a physical education program is a misuse of fitness testing.

Pedometers provide authentic evaluation of daily physical activity that can be used to identify inactive youth and reward those who increase their activity levels. Becoming more active creates goodwill among students, parents, teachers, and administrators. Who wouldn't want to graduate students who have a positive attitude toward physical activity and know how to evaluate their personal levels of daily activity? Parents appreciate teachers who help their children develop and maintain a healthy lifestyle.

An innovative way to foster this positive activity-based culture is through the creation and promotion of healthy and active school environments. Data support that physically active youth have a better chance of becoming active adults, thus paving the way for a healthier society (Raitakari, et al., 1994; Telama, et al., 1997). To do this only in physical education, where fewer than 2,000 steps of 6- to 12-year-old boys' and girls' mean total daily step counts (12,554 to 13,872 and 10,661 to 11,383, respectively) are accumulated would be ineffective (Morgan, Pangrazi, & Beighle, 2003). Throughout the rest of the school day and outside of school, approximately 8,000 to 11,000 more steps are accumulated. Thus, creating a healthy and supportive school environment conducive to physical activity throughout the day has the potential to play an important role in the activity levels of youth.

Reinforcing this new approach to health that focuses on the school environment was the enactment in the United States of the Child Nutrition and WIC Reauthorization Act of 2004, which requires schools participating in the U.S. Department of Agriculture child nutrition programs to implement a four-component local wellness policy. Physical activity, nutrition education, nutrition standards for on-campus foods, and school-based wellness activities must be developed and implemented through the collaborative work of students, parents, school boards, school administrators, and the public. The timing of this influential act may be just the impetus needed to create a shift in thinking toward a broader view of the school environment, that is, creating a culture that changes children's activity behaviors and attitudes. Examples of how to create a healthy and active school environment include the following: offering physical activity programs during and after school, posting signs and creating newsletters promoting physical activity, and enhancing the "walkability" of the environment to and from school. For more examples and activities see www.activeandhealthyschools.com. In addition, a comprehensive physical activity program that encourages students to earn the Presidential Active Lifestyle Award (PALA) and schools to become an Active Lifestyle Model School (www.presidentschallenge.org) offers highly visible evidence that activity is a critical component of the total school environment.

Final Thoughts

The primary focus of this book is to provide creative ways for teachers and students in public and private schools and universities to increase their physical activity and to determine the most effective ways to create healthy and active school environments that meet their needs. To do this, the use of a small, objective measurement device, the pedometer, can motivate, help students self-monitor, provide feedback, and measure levels of physical activity in terms of steps and activity time. An additional purpose of this book is to facilitate the accountability shift to total volume of daily physical activity accumulated through the use of digital pedometers. Pedometers can be used as a low-cost, accurate, and personal method to evaluate and teach students to be active. For an inactive youngster who dislikes physical activity, the pedometer can bring about positive changes in attitudes and behavior that can lead to healthy lifestyles in the future. The pedometer is easy to use, nonthreatening, private (no one has to see how many steps another person has taken), and able to gather physical activity data throughout the day. Its use as an accurate and meaningful data collection and motivational tool has been well supported in research, and this book helps practitioners put this research to practice with its easy-to-read format and practical examples.

If You Want to Know More . . .

The following Web sites are helpful if you want to know more about the topics in this chapter. They contain information that is constantly updated and revised. Many of the government Web sites are useful because they present current survey data and information for improving everyday health.

Web Sites

www.presidentschallenge.org

The President's Challenge site provides information about physical fitness and the Presidential Active Lifestyle Awards.

www.health.gov/healthypeople

This site provides information on America's goals for Healthy People 2010, including recent revisions to the goals.

www.cdc.gov

Centers for Disease Control and Prevention's site offers a wide variety of information related to health, physical activity, and substance abuse.

www.pecentral.org

PE Central is a Web site for health and physical education teachers that includes a number of lesson plans for pedometers and physical activity.

www.cdc.gov/HealthyYouth/CSHP

This site details the eight-component model for coordinated school health programs.

www.cdc.gov/nccdphp/sgr/adoles.htm

This site contains a basic fact sheet about adolescents and the effects of physical activity on their health.

www.activeandhealthyschools.com

The Active and Healthy Schools Program is a program from Gopher Sport and The President's Challenge.

www.beactive.com.au

This site from the South Australia Physical Activity Council promotes active lifestyles for citizens of all ages.

www.healthyactive.gov.au

This site for Building a Healthy, Active Australia offers information and strategies for healthy eating, school and community coalitions, and active after-school programs.

www.activeliving.ca

Canada's Web site for Coalition for Active Living lists many guidelines and policy statements for health and physical activity.

www.activehealthykids.ca

Canada's site for creating active and healthy children places strong emphasis on physical activity rather than physical fitness strategies.

References

Bailey, R.C., Olson, J., Pepper, S.L., Porszaz, J., Barstow, T.J., & Cooper, D.M. (1995). The level and tempo of children's physical activities: An observational study. *Medicine and Science in Sports and Exercise, 27*(7), 1033-1041.

Bar-Or, O., Foreyt, J., Bouchard, C., et al. (1998). Physical activity, genetic, and nutritional considerations in childhood weight management. *Medicine and Science in Sports and Exercise, 30*(1), 2-10.

Beighle, A. & Pangrazi, R.P. (2006). Measuring children's activity levels: The association between step-counts and activity time. *Journal of Physical Activity and Health, 3*(2), 221-229.

Beighle, A., Pangrazi, R.P., & Vincent, S.D. (2001). Pedometers, physical activity, and accountability. *Journal of Physical Education, Recreation and Dance, 72*(9), 16-36.

Blair, S.N. & Brodney, S. (1999). Effects of physical inactivity and obesity on morbidity and mortality: Current evidence and research issues. *Medicine and Science in Sports and Exercise, 31*(11 Suppl.), S646-S662.

Blair, S.N., Kohl, H.W., Barlow, C.E., Paffenbarger, R.S., Gibbons, L.W., & Macera, C.A. (1995). Changes in physical fitness and all-cause mortality: A prospective study of healthy and unhealthy men. *Journal of the American Medical Association, 273*(14), 1093-1098.

Bouchard, C. (1999). Heredity and health-related fitness. In C.B. Corbin & R.P. Pangrazi (Eds.), *Toward a Better Understanding of Physical Fitness and Activity* (pp. 11-17). Scottsdale, AZ: Holcomb Hathaway.

Chan, C.B., Spangler, E., Valcour, J., & Tudor-Locke, C. (2003). Cross-sectional relationship of pedometer-determined ambulatory activity to indicators of health. *Obesity Research, 11*(12), 1563-1570.

Corbin, C.B., & Pangrazi, R.P. (1992). Are American children and youth fit? *Research Quarterly for Exercise and Sport, 63*, 96-116.

Corbin, C.B., Welk, G.J., Corbin, W.R., & Welk, K.A. (2008). *Concepts of fitness and wellness: A comprehensive lifestyle approach* (7th ed.). Boston: McGraw-Hill.

Dunn, A.L., Andersen, R.E., & Jakicic, J.M. (1998). Lifestyle physical activity interventions. *American Journal of Preventive Medicine, 15*(4), 398-412.

Dunn, A.L., Marcus, B.H., Kampert, J.B., Garcia, M.E., Kohl, H.W., & Blair, S.N. (1999). Comparison of lifestyle and structured interventions to increase physical activity and cardiorespiratory fitness: A randomized trial. *Journal of the American Medical Association, 281*(4), 327-334.

Haskell, W.L. (1994). Health consequences of physical activity: Understanding and challenges regarding dose-response. *Medicine and Science in Sports and Exercise, 26*(6), 649-660.

Hopple, C. & Graham, G. (1995). What children think, feel, and know about physical fitness testing. *Journal of Teaching in Physical Education, 14*, 408-417.

Hornbuckle, L.M., Bassett, D.R., & Thompson, D.L. (2005). Pedometer-determined walking and body composition variables in African-American women. *Medicine and Science in Sports and Exercise, 37*(6), 1069-1074.

Le Masurier, C., Beighle, A., Corbin, C., Darst, P.W., Morgan, C.F., Pangrazi, R.P., Vincent, S., & Wilde, B. (2005). Pedometer-determined physical activity levels of youth. *Journal of Physical Activity and Health, 2*(2), 159-168.

Malina, R.M. (1996). Tracking of physical activity and physical fitness across the lifespan. *Research Quarterly for Exercise and Sport, 67,* 48-57.

Morgan, C.F., Pangrazi, R.P., & Beighle, A. (2003). Using pedometers to promote physical activity in physical education. *Journal of Physical Education, Recreation and Dance, 74*(7), 33-38.

National Association for Sport and Physical Education. (2004). *Physical activity for children: A statement of guidelines* (2nd ed.). Reston, VA: Author.

Paffenbarger, R.S., Hyde, R.T., Wing, A.L., & Hsieh, C.C. (1986). Physical activity, all-cause mortality, and longevity of college alumni. *New England Journal of Medicine, 314,* 605-613.

Pangrazi, R.P., Corbin, C.B., & Welk, G.J. (1996). Physical activity for children and youth. *Journal of Physical Education, Recreation and Dance, 67*(4), 38-43.

President's Council on Physical Fitness and Sports. (2006). *The president's challenge handbook.* Washington, DC: Author.

Raitakari, O.T., Porkka, K.V., Viikari, J.S., Ronnemaa, T., & Akerblom, H.K. (1994). Clustering of risk factors for coronary heart disease in children and adolescents. The Cardiovascular Risk in Young Finns Study, *Acta Paediatric, 83*(9), 935-940.

Rowlands, A.V. & Eston, R.G. (2005). Comparison of accelerometer and pedometer measures of physical activity in boys and girls, ages 8-10 years, *Research Quarterly for Exercise and Sport, 76*(3), 251-257.

Sallis, J.F. & McKenzie, T.L. (1991). Physical education's role in public health. *Research Quarterly for Exercise and Sport, 62*(2), 124-137.

Sallis, J.F., & Patrick, K. (1994). Physical activity guidelines for adolescents: Consensus statement. *Pediatric Exercise Science, 6*(4), 302-314.

Scruggs, P.W., Beveridge, S.K, Eisenman, P.A., Watson, D.L., Shultz, B.B., & Ransdell, L.B. (2003). Quantifying physical activity via pedometry in elementary physical education. *Medicine and Science in Sports and Exercise, 35*(6), 1065-1071.

Strong, W.B., Malina, R.M., Blimkie, C.J., et al. (2005). Evidence-based physical activity for school-age youth. *Journal of Pediatrics, 146,* 732-737.

Telama, R., Yang, X., Laakso, L., & Viikari, J. (1997). Physical activity in childhood and adolescence as predictor of physical activity in adulthood. *American Journal of Preventive Medicine, 13*(4), 317-323.

Thompson, A.M., Baxter-Jones, A.D.G., Mirwald, R.L, & Bailey, D.A. (2003). Comparison of physical activity in male and female children: Does maturation matter? *Medicine and Science in Sports and Exercise, 35*(10), 1684-1690.

Thompson, D.L., Rakow, J., & Perdue, S.M. (2004). Relationship between accumulated walking and body composition in middle-aged women. *Medicine and Science in Sports and Exercise, 36*(5), 911-914.

Tudor-Locke, C., Lee, S.M., Morgan, C.F., Beighle, A., & Pangrazi, R.P. (2006). Children's pedometer-determined physical activity patterns during the segmented school day. *Medicine and Science in Sports and Exercise, 38*(1), 1732-1738.

Tudor-Locke, C.E., Pangrazi, R.P., Corbin, C.B., Rutherford, W.J., Vincent, S.D., Raustorp, A., Tomson, L.M., & Cuddihy, T.F. (2004). BMI-referenced standards for recommended pedometer-determined steps/day in children. *Preventive Medicine, 38,* 857-864.

U.S. Department of Health and Human Services. (1996). *Physical activity and health: A report of the Surgeon General.* U.S. Department of Health and Human Services, Centers for Disease Control and Prevention, and National Center for Chronic Disease Prevention and Health Promotion. (Eds.). Atlanta: Author.

U.S. Department of Health and Human Services. (1998). Healthy People 2010: Physical activity & health, chapter 22. Retrieved November 18, 2006 from www.healthypeople.gov/Document/HTML/Volume2/22Physical.htm.

Vincent, S.D., Pangrazi, R.P., Raustorp, A., Tomson, L.M., & Cuddihy, T.F. (2003). Activity levels and body mass index of children in the United States, Sweden, and Australia. *Medicine and Science in Sports and Exercise, 35*(8), 1367-1373.

Whitaker, R.C., Wright, J.A., Pepe, M.S., et al. (1997). Predicting obesity in young adulthood from childhood and parental obesity. *New England Journal of Medicine, 337*(13), 869-873.

Funding, Purchasing, and Managing Pedometers

The previous chapter provided a rationale for promoting physical activity and introduced research suggesting that pedometer-measured physical activity has numerous health benefits. This chapter focuses on administrative information associated with using pedometers. To maximize the effectiveness of using pedometers to promote physical activity, several steps must be taken. Plans for initial and continued funding, knowledge about the types of pedometers that are available, and strategies for managing pedometers once they are purchased are necessary.

Funding

For many schools, the money to purchase pedometers may not be available in the physical education budget or even in the school's budget. Therefore, a person must be identified who is creative, persistent, and patient in trying to obtain pedometers. This individual, most often the physical education teacher, should have the responsibility for making physical activity a priority for all children. Even if a school already has pedometers, it is important to constantly seek funding to replace pedometers, purchase batteries, and acquire additional pedometers for new students. The following sources, opportunities, and means for obtaining pedometers are available to most schools.

Local Businesses

Local businesses are often willing to support schools in their area. Donating to schools not only creates positive public relations, but it also serves as a productive form of advertising. For physical education to benefit from the generosity of local businesses, three steps are necessary.

1. Contact the business owners with a phone call, letter, or, preferably, a face-to-face meeting.
2. Show the business owners the benefits of funding pedometers for the school, in terms of both promoting physical activity for students and positive public relations. Offer a brief handout and discussion that explains how pedometers are used to promote lifestyle activity. Discuss how using pedometers benefits the school, community, and, most important, their business. Information for preparing such a handout can be drawn from experience and chapters in this book.
3. Invite the business owners to visit the school and participate in a physical education lesson that incorporates pedometers. If pedometers are not available, explain to the business leader how they would be used if funding were available. Getting adults to

participate in a lesson is an effective way to communicate the importance of a high-quality physical education program.

Persistence is critical. This effort may require meeting with numerous business owners and hearing "no" repeatedly. However, exposing business leaders to high-quality physical education will build bridges that pay off in the future.

Parent–Teacher Organizations

Parent organizations, such as PTA and school booster clubs, are often a rich source of funding. As with businesses, receiving money from parent organizations requires extensive preliminary work. A relationship can be developed with members of the organization by attending meetings, helping with fund-raisers, and offering positive feedback about the school. Another avenue for developing rapport with parents in the community is to hold Physical Education Nights. These nights can be staged with students demonstrating the program (e.g., Physical Education Demo Night) or with parents and students participating together (e.g., Family Night). For a detailed description of these events, see Morgan and Morgan, 2004. Not all students in the school can meet on the same evening, so staggering these events for different grade levels throughout the year is an effective way to develop public relations with parents.

Once a relationship is established and parents know about the physical education program at their child's school, the next step is to ask for a few minutes at one of the organization's meetings to request funding for pedometers. Make a short presentation that explains the benefits of physical activity and how pedometers in physical education can help promote lifestyle activity. (See the Pedometer Presentation Outline on page 24 for an example.) During this presentation, stress to parents that pedometers are being requested to benefit their children now as well as in the future.

Universities

Because pedometers are an efficient way to measure physical activity, many universities are beginning to use them for research. One critical component of carrying out successful research studies is recruitment of people willing to participate. Researchers may be interested in studying students, their parents, other adults (teachers, staff), or a combination of these populations. Contact local universities, specifically physical education departments (other departmental names include kinesiology, exercise science, exercise and wellness, health, and public health), to see if they would like to conduct research in a school setting. Researchers are willing to compensate participants or those who recruit participants

Pedometer Presentation Outline

I. Personal introduction

II. Shifting paradigm in physical education

    a. Fitness testing

        i. Use

        ii. Limitations

    b. Promoting lifestyle activity as the focus of physical education

    c. Need for physical activity

        i. Decreasing all-cause mortality

        ii. Children's activity tracks

III. Measuring physical activity

    a. Brief discussion of all methods

    b. Pedometer most feasible

        i. Cost

        ii. Unobtrusive

        iii. Reliable and valid

IV. Uses of pedometers

    a. Teach students

    b. Improve teaching

    c. Improve program

During this portion of the presentation, the specific benefits of pedometer use for the audience are included.

V. Specific needs

    a. Number of pedometers and why

    b. Cost per pedometer and total cost

    c. Maintenance

VI. Questions?

VII. Thank the audience for their time and consideration

From Robert P. Pangrazi, Aaron Beighle, and Cara L. Sidman, 2007, *Pedometer Power, Second Edition*, (Champaign, IL: Human Kinetics).

(e.g., physical education teachers) for studies. Many have access to an abundance of pedometers through grants, university funds, and other sources. Thus, one method for compensating participants can be to donate pedometers.

Getting money from one organization, even if it is not enough for a full set of pedometers, is a good start. Combining donations from more than one source is acceptable and is often necessary. When attempting to secure funds for the purchase of pedometers, do not be discouraged by rejection. A proposal and agreement need to be developed over time, and people usually resist the first or second request. There are many options. With determination and imagination, it is possible to generate the funds necessary to purchase pedometers.

Grants

Grants are an excellent source of funding. Many people are intimidated by the notion of writing a proposal for a grant. However, many sources of assistance are available for grant writing. Many school districts have grant writers, and faculty members from local universities may have grant-writing experience and be willing to assist. It is becoming more common for teachers to apply for grants, meaning it is likely that at least one teacher in a school has applied for a grant or developed a grant proposal. Working with experienced colleagues not only distributes the labor, but it also increases the likelihood of success in receiving a grant.

Another misconception about grants is that they are only awarded to large universities or hospitals. Resources intended to provide funds for individual teachers or programs are available. Many health departments offer minigrants for school-based programs designed to improve the health of children. County 4-H programs and university outreach programs are common. The state of Virginia has teamed up with Walk4life, a pedometer company, to develop the WalkSmart, Virginia! program. This pedometer-based incentive program is designed to increase physical activity levels of fourth, seventh, and ninth graders. Students wear pedometers and log their steps into an Internet-based application each day. The software takes them on a virtual tour of the state (based on their accumulation of steps), offering students a view of important events and locations. This application combines academic concepts with physical activity, which results in a total-school approach to learning. If teachers in Virginia are willing to take the lead in implementing this program, the pedometers are supplied. The WalkSmart! ActiveSchools program is now available for all states in the United States. The hope is that many more states and countries will adopt similar programs to help attenuate the obesity epidemic engulfing the population. With hard work, teamwork, and digging, sources for funding are available and can be secured.

Purchasing

Once the question of "Where am I going to get the money?" is answered, numerous other questions arise. How many pedometers are needed? Are all of the functions necessary? This section provides the answers to these questions and helps readers make educated decisions when selecting pedometers. Before acquiring or requesting funding, the following questions should be answered to help estimate how much money is needed.

How Many Pedometers Should I Purchase?

When purchasing pedometers for physical education, class size is the critical factor. Ideally there should be one pedometer for each student in the class. Although the activities in this book can be adapted for classes with one pedometer for every two or three students, it is best for each student to have a pedometer. Most likely, because of cost, one set of pedometers will be purchased and rotated between classes.

As with any piece of equipment, the long-term goal is to accumulate an adequate number of pedometers so that they can be used in many different situations, including after-school and overnight recording of physical activity. Therefore, the number of pedometers should exceed the number of students in the largest physical education class. We suggest that pedometer purchases be based on the largest class size plus 20 percent to cover loss, breakage, and theft. In other words, for a class of 30 students, purchase at least 36 pedometers.

What Functions Are Necessary?

The basic function found on all pedometers is step counting. However, other functions can increase the utility of pedometers. One function that is opening many doors for research and physical activity promotion is activity time. A relatively new function to pedometers is their ability to assess the amount of time a person spends taking steps, or essentially, being active. While the pedometer's lever arm is moving to count steps, an internal stopwatch is accumulating time. When the lever arm stops, the stopwatch stops. Thus, at the conclusion of a day, the pedometer might read 8,542 steps and 1:20:42 of activity time. This means that it took the person one hour, 20 minutes, and 42 seconds to take 8,542 steps.

Measuring physical activity time rather than steps is useful for a variety of reasons. One, it eliminates the influence of stride length on measured activity. For example, if a short child and a tall child walk together for 20 minutes, the shorter child is likely to take more steps because he or she has a smaller stride length. This may seem unfair and cause frustration for the taller child. However, at the end of the walk, both children will have accumulated 20 minutes of activity time. Activity time negates these physiological differences, which makes it easier to set goals for a class of students. Another example applies to measuring physical activity during physical education. If a taller obese student and a shorter lean student wear pedometers and each moves for 20 minutes during a 30-minute lesson, both can feel successful in the amount of activity they achieved even though the shorter student most likely accumulated more steps. Again, if steps were the only measurement, it might be discouraging for the taller obese student who worked equally hard, but did not take as many steps.

Using a cost-effective tool such as pedometers to assess activity time allows teachers and students to compare their daily physical activity to national goals and recommendations. Healthy People 2010 recommends children be active during at least 50 percent of their physical education lesson. Before the development of this pedometer feature, labor-intensive direct observation and the use of more-costly accelerometers or heart rate monitors were the only means by which to assess minutes of physical activity. As discussed in chapter 1, many of the physical activity recommendations for youth are in minutes, thus being able to use pedometers to assess minutes of activity makes goal setting easy for students and parents to understand.

Finally, the activity-time feature, combined with the simultaneous measurement of steps, allows for the calculation of steps per minute (SPM). This variable has many potentially practical applications. First, as SPM increases, one could argue that physical activity intensity increases. For example, a child who averages 92 SPM over the course of a day, on average, is active at a lower intensity than a child who averages 100 SPM. Current research is underway to determine how many steps per minute need to be attained to bring activity up to the moderate to vigorous level.

Similarly, measuring SPM allows researchers to assess the relationship between steps and activity time. For example, Beighle and Pangrazi (2006) developed a regression equation that predicts minutes of physical activity from steps. Practically speaking, teachers who only have pedometers that can assess steps can convert steps into minutes of physical activity using this equation. It is important to point out that this equation is for daily physical activity only and does not apply to physical education activity. Because of the duration and structure of physical education, it would be expected that students would accumulate more steps per minute during physical education, but studies examining this specific question using activity time as measured by pedometers is still needed. Recently, a study was done calculating SPM as physical education steps per total lesson time (Scruggs et al., 2003). This calculation provided lower numbers than reported in preliminary work reported elsewhere (Morgan, Pangrazi, & Beighle, 2005). Although SPM is a promising variable to measure, research is needed before drawing conclusions regarding its utility. Stride length increases with age. How does stride length affect SPM? Do SPM values differ during physical education and everyday activities during the rest of the day? Does weight affect SPM? These are just a few of the exciting questions that must be addressed to maximize the use of the activity-time function of pedometers.

Numerous pedometers are on the market, and as with any product, the quality varies depending on the manufacturer and cost. In recent years, many valid and reliable pedometers have become available (Beets, Patton, & Edwards, 2005; Schneider, Crouter, Lukajic, & Bassett, 2003), thus providing many options for the buyer. When choosing a pedometer, first ensure that the pedometer is accurate. The best way to determine this is to examine the research. The accuracy of certain pedometer models and features has been researched, while others have not yet undergone investigation (Bassett et al., 1996). For fieldwork (free-living activity), pedometers that are accurate within 10 percent are deemed acceptable (Rowe, Mahar, Raedeke, & Lore, 2004). In fact, an efficient way to test the accuracy of the pedometers is to perform a simple shake test, in which the pedometers are manually moved up and down in a box for a specified number of times and then checked for how close the recording is to the actual number of shakes (see page 30, Checking for Accuracy) (Vincent & Sidman, 2003).

Other ways to evaluate the quality of the pedometer is by considering the cost and features. Pedometers that are given away by fast-food restaurants or can be purchased for a few dollars at a sporting goods store are not likely to be of high quality. Most of the pedometers that have been validated by research offer numerous features including steps, distance, activity time, and calories or kilojoules expended. Usually, pedometers that assess distance and energy expended are not recommended for elementary-age children. First, entering body weight and stride length to calculate these variables is time consuming and cumbersome. Second, for a variety of reasons, the information received is not as accurately reported as are steps and time. Third, when there are several functions on the pedometer, youngsters often have difficulty telling which function they are using. Lastly, if distance is desired, physical educators can collaborate with a classroom teacher and have the students measure their stride length and calculate the distance traveled as part of a math lesson. Another feature on pedometers that is particularly useful in physical education is a three-second–delay reset. No matter how cautious students are, inevitably the reset button will inadvertently be hit and data lost. The three-second delay eliminates this issue by requiring a conscious, sustained effort to reset the pedometer. With the wide price ranges and features, it is important for the physical educator to weigh the costs with the benefits in order to choose the best pedometer.

A common concern raised by teachers is the amount of time it takes students to put pedometers on at the beginning of class. With improperly sized clothes, large waistbands, and lack of fine motor skills for some students, this is a legitimate concern. To ease this problem and allow pedometers to be put on quickly, some pedometers offer an alligator clip (see figure 2.1). With this clasp, students can quickly squeeze the clip, place the pedometer in the appropriate location (see chapter 3), and be ready for action. However, it is important to remember that pedometers that go on easily also come off easily. If possible, it may be best to have a few alligator clip pedometers available for students who are unable to put the pedometer on in a timely manner or are wearing pants with a thick waistband.

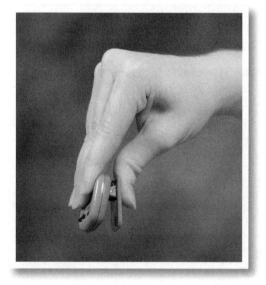

Figure 2.1   Sample alligator clip.

How Much Should I Pay for Pedometers?

Prices for pedometers range from $24 for one pedometer to as low as $8 to $12 each when large quantities are purchased. Bells and whistles may increase the price—from $20 pedometers on TV infomercials to $40 counters with compasses and clocks designed for hikers. (Prices are stated in U.S. dollars.) Costs increase with the addition of supplementary items such as teacher kits, special containers, and safety straps to prevent dropping. Ideally, you will be able to purchase the most accurate pedometers that possess the features that best suit your needs at the lowest possible price.

Managing

Funding has been secured and the pedometers have been purchased, now what? To ensure accuracy of the pedometers, minimize loss, and maximize their use in your school, it is highly recommended that you develop a pedometer management protocol.

Maintaining Pedometers

As with any mechanical device, pedometers require maintenance. Fortunately, the maintenance is minimal. It requires periodically checking the pedometers for accuracy and changing the batteries. These two tasks are quick and easy to perform. Older, more responsible students may be trained to assist with these tests.

Checking for Accuracy

Pedometers should be checked for accuracy when they are purchased, followed by yearly checks when equipment inventory is taken. One method of checking for accuracy is the "shake test." This test involves using the small plastic storage box seen in figure 2.2. These boxes can be purchased at most discount retail stores. The following is the procedure for conducting a shake test.

1. Reset all pedometers and place them vertically in the box. Two pedometers will fit in each "pocket."
2. Close the lid and use a rubber band to secure it.
3. Gently move the box up and down with a cadence similar to brisk walking. Shake it 30 to 50 times.
4. Check the pedometers for accuracy. The acceptable error rate for the shake test is plus or minus 3 percent. An inaccurate pedometer may need new batteries or repair.
5. Repeat the test two or three times before drawing conclusions.

Another method of checking pedometers for accuracy is a "walk test." This test involves wearing a pedometer and walking a set number of steps. The "walk test" is performed as follows:

1. Fasten a pedometer to the waistband.
2. Reset the pedometer.
3. Take 30 steps.
4. On the 30th step, stop and record the number of steps taken.

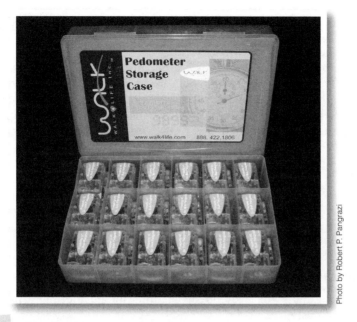

Photo by Robert P. Pangrazi

Figure 2.2   Plastic pedometer storage box.

An acceptable error rate for pedometers worn at the waist during the walk test is 10 percent or less. Perform the test two or three times for each pedometer.

Changing Batteries

Pedometers are powered by small, watch-type batteries. Generally, the battery placed in the pedometer by the manufacturer will last approximately two years. Before changing batteries, perform an accuracy test and purchase batteries accordingly. To determine the type of battery needed and how to change it, consult the pedometer's manufacturer or distributor or the operating instructions that may have come with the pedometer. If the pedometer remains inaccurate after the battery is replaced, consult the distributor.

Using Pedometers Outside of the Physical Education Environment

A long-term goal for pedometer use is to involve the entire school community—teachers, staff, and families. To accomplish this goal, program administrators must allow pedometers to be taken out of the confines of the physical education class. Pedometers can be worn before school, during school, and after school. They also can be taken home to share with family members. However, allowing pedometers to be used outside the school opens the door to loss and damage. For this reason, we recommend that only those students who have used pedometers responsibly during physical education classes for two to three months should be permitted to check them out to take home. To minimize loss, institute a checkout system. This will help track who was using a pedometer when it was lost, damaged, or stolen.

The pedometer checkout system involves at least two situations: checking out a pedometer during the school day and checking out a pedometer to take home. Both of these situations require adult supervision and the establishment of a designated pedometer checkout area (e.g., the physical education office). Beyond these two situations, schools may need additional procedures for tracking pedometers.

Checking Out a Pedometer for the School Day

The following steps provide suggestions for developing a pedometer checkout system.

1. Create a pedometer checkout form (see page 33).
2. Designate an area in the school where students go to check out pedometers. The physical education office or the media center is a good choice.
3. For each time period that students can check out pedometers (e.g., before school, during lunch, and after school), create a new checkout form. Another possibility is to include time periods on the same form. However, if the same pedometer is checked out by different students before school and after school, a new sheet for each time period will eliminate confusion.
4. After each checkout time, inventory the pedometers and question students about missing, lost, or damaged pedometers.
5. Keep all checkout sheets on file, particularly if there are not enough pedometers for all the students who wish to check them out. Filed checkout sheets can then be used to ensure that all students have equal opportunity to use the pedometers. A rotation by grade can ensure equitable distribution of pedometers to all students.

If another adult (e.g., an aide or the media specialist) will monitor pedometer checkout, familiarize this person with the procedure. Responsible students can help with the checkout procedure; however, the presence of an adult is essential, especially in the initial phases.

Pedometer Checkout Form

Date _____

Ped. #	Morning		Lunch		After school	
	Student	Staff initials (In/Out)	Student	Staff initials (In/Out)	Student	Staff initials (In/Out)
1						
2						
3						
4						
5						
6						
7						
8						
9						
10						
11						
12						
13						
14						
15						
16						
17						
18						
19						
20						
21						
22						
23						
24						
25						
26						
27						
28						
29						
30						
31						

From Robert P. Pangrazi, Aaron Beighle, and Cara L. Sidman, 2007, *Pedometer Power, Second Edition*, (Champaign, IL: Human Kinetics).

Checking Out a Pedometer to Take Home

Allowing students to take pedometers home can produce positive results. The family environment is an important factor in a student's decision to be physically active (Brustad, 1993, 1996; Kimiecik & Horn, 1998; Freedson & Evenson, 1991). Exposure to pedometers has the potential to involve the entire family in lifestyle physical activity. However, along with these potentially positive developments comes the challenge of preventing lost pedometers. Allowing students to take pedometers home necessitates careful monitoring to minimize loss. One way to minimize loss is to limit the amount of time pedometers can be checked out to one night or one weekend. The teacher or person responsible for the pedometers should be the only person to check out pedometers to students for use overnight or for a weekend. Pedometers should not be taken home without a parent's or guardian's prior knowledge. Create a permission slip that the student's parent or guardian signs. The permission slip should include the following:

- A paragraph about pedometers that explains why the student will bring it home and that encourages the parents to talk to the student about physical activity.
- A paragraph explaining how to care for the pedometer.
- A statement holding the parent or student financially accountable if the pedometer is not returned or is damaged beyond the normally expected scratches and cracks. Extensive damage to the case or the mechanisms inside is not considered reasonable damage.

Some teachers may find greater security in requiring parents to come to the school to check out the pedometers. However, if parental involvement at a school is low, this method will decrease the number of students who have access to a pedometer at home. The same permission slip can be used with this method.

Final Thoughts

When considering implementation of a pedometer program for your school, whether it be for physical education classes or after-school programs, careful thought regarding pedometer features, type, cost, and proper use is strongly recommended. A good place to start is to determine if research has been conducted on the accuracy and usefulness of the pedometer in question and if the population with whom you are working has been investigated. Inevitably there will be challenges regarding funding, purchasing, and managing pedometers, but by using the information presented in this chapter, the process can certainly be facilitated.

If You Want to Know More . . .

These sites offer helpful information about funding, purchasing, and managing pedometers. When purchasing pedometers in large quantities, always contact the vendors to see if a better price can be negotiated.

Web Sites

www.aahperd.org/NASPE/template.cfm?template=grant_opp.html

This site details grant opportunities that are available from the National Association for Sport and Physical Education.

www.pelinks4u.org/naspeforum/discus/messages/7/529.html
?1120146903

This site contains the National Association for Sport and Physical Education forum on grant writing.

www.cdc.gov/youthcampaign/materials/adults/active_children.htm

This site offers an excellent brochure, *Active Children, Active Families,* developed by the Centers for Disease Control and Prevention.

www.walk4life.com

This site features Walk4life pedometers and related instructional materials for teachers, families, and health providers.

www.pelinks4u.org

The PE Links site has a strong focus on physical activity and health and changing directions in the profession.

www.pecentral.org

PE Central is a Web site for health and physical education.

www.walksmartactiveschools.com/default_pages/default_home.aspx

The WalkSmart! Active Schools site explains how to log activity and integrate academic concepts through a Web-based program.

www.excelway.ca

This CAHPERD site is an online center for teaching resources and equipment.

www.livingschool.ca

This site features the Ontario Physical and Health Education Association (OPHEA) initiative promoting healthy, active, open school communities.

www.sainsburys.co.uk/activekids
www.tesco.com/sport/

In the UK, supermarkets such as Sainsbury's and Tesco run annual promotions in which they provide vouchers that could help fund pedometer programs.

References

Bassett, D.R., Ainsworth, B.E., Leggett, S.R., Mathien, C.A., Main, J.A., Hunter, D.C., & Duncan, G.E. (1996). Accuracy of five electronic pedometers for measuring distance walked. *Medicine and Science in Sports and Exercise, 28*(8), 1071-1077.

Beets, M., Patton, M.M., & Edwards, S. (2005). The accuracy of pedometer steps and time during walking in children. *Medicine and Science in Sports and Exercise, 37*(3), 513-520.

Beighle, A. & Pangrazi, R.P. (2006). Measuring children's activity levels: The association between step-counts and activity time. *Journal of Physical Activity and Health, 3*(2), 221-229.

Brustad, R.J. (1993). Who will go out and play? Parental and psychological influences on children's attraction to physical activity. *Pediatric Exercise Science, 5*, 210-223.

Brustad, R.J. (1996). Attraction to physical activity in urban schoolchildren: Parental socialization and gender influences. *Research Quarterly for Exercise and Sport, 67*, 316-323.

Freedson, P.S. & Evenson, S. (1991). Familial aggregation in physical activity. *Research Quarterly for Exercise and Sport, 62*, 384-389.

Kimiecik, J.C. & Horn, T.S. (1998). Parental beliefs and children's moderate-to-vigorous physical activity. *Research Quarterly for Exercise and Sport, 69*, 163-175.

Morgan, C.L., & Morgan, C.F. (2004). Promoting physical activity: Physical education nights. *Teaching Elementary Physical Education, 15*(5), 33-35.

Morgan, C.F., Pangrazi, R.P., & Beighle, A. (2005). Does physical education benefit the least active children? *Research Quarterly for Sport and Exercise, 76*(1 Suppl.), A-84.

Rowe, D.A., Mahar, M.T., Raedeke, T.D., & Lore, J. (2004). Measuring physical activity in children with pedometers: Reliability, reactivity, and replacement of missing data. *Pediatric Exercise Science, 16*(4), 343-354.

Schneider, P.L., Crouter, S.E., Lukajic, O., & Bassett, D.R. (2003). Accuracy and reliability of 10 pedometers for measuring steps over 400-m walk. *Medicine and Science in Sports and Exercise, 35*, 1779-1784.

Scruggs, P.W., Beveridge, S.K., Eisenman, P.A., Watson, D.L., Shultz, B.B., & Ransdell, L.B. (2003). Quantifying physical activity via pedometry in elementary physical education. *Medicine and Science in Sports and Exercise, 35*(6), 1065-1071.

Vincent, S.D. & Sidman, C.L. (2003). Determining measurement error in digital pedometers. *Measurement in Physical Education and Exercise Science, 7*(1), 19-24.

Using Pedometers
in Physical Education

When used properly, pedometers can be a valuable tool for teaching students about the importance of lifestyle physical activity. This chapter includes information on how to introduce pedometers to students, find the most accurate pedometer placement for each student, and how to manage pedometer use by developing efficient class routines. Ideas for collecting pedometer data by having students record their own data are presented along with strategies for using pedometer data to improve physical education instruction.

Introducing Pedometers to Students

Most likely, physical education teachers will be responsible for introducing pedometers to students. Introduce them to classes that are able to quickly adapt to new ideas. Such a class offers an opportunity to test and refine the process and to work out problems before presenting pedometers to other classes. When first introducing students to a pedometer, they need to know what it is, how it works, and how to wear it. As with all new gadgets, students will want to "explore" the pedometer during the first few uses. Initial lessons should provide students with a chance to become accustomed to the novel device. When developing a plan for introducing pedometers, do the following:

1. Establish guidelines for use. Some students may shake the pedometer to artificially increase step counts and activity time. A consequence is needed to prevent this behavior. "You shake it, we take it" (i.e., losing the privilege of using the pedometer) is an effective deterrent.

2. Discuss how pedometers work, including why they are suitable for physical education. To hold the interest of the students, keep the introduction short, about two to three minutes. If necessary, break up a long discussion by allowing students to try the pedometers and come back later for more instruction.

3. After the brief discussion, distribute the pedometers to the class. Encourage the students, under supervision only, to satisfy their curiosity about the pedometers. Let them open the devices, shake, reset, and listen to them.

4. Teach students how to place the pedometers on their bodies. Provide pedometer belts to students who wear dresses, overalls, or other types of beltless garments. Nylon belts similar to the type used for football flags work very well and are easy to make. A related guideline for students is "once the pedometer is on, it does not come off until you are instructed to take it off." The pedometer does not have to be taken off to view results. If students

keep taking the pedometer off, it will be distracting to others, and the chances of pedometers being dropped and broken increase.

5. Once students have the pedometers properly attached to their waists, have them walk around the teaching area. They can stop and open the pedometer (without taking it off) to see if it is working correctly.

6. Finally, have the students engage in a few teacher-directed games while wearing the pedometers. While participating in activities, have students periodically read their pedometers to check their activity level. Let students know that pedometer steps and activity time are private and personal, and they have no obligation to share their data with their peers. Figure 3.1 offers discussion points to cover when introducing pedometers to a class.

Finding an Accurate Placement Point for the Pedometer

Once pedometers have been introduced and students know how to use them, the next step is to find an accurate pedometer placement for each student. Generally, placing the pedometer on the waist, directly above the knee is the best location. Although most students will find this placement to be accurate, some students may not because of their body type and gait. For example, if an obese child wears the pedometer directly over the knee, excess body fat may force the pedometer to rest at an angle that is not parallel to the body plane. If the pedometer is not upright and parallel to the body, it will not assess steps or time accurately. Undercounting steps, particularly for an obese child, can be discouraging during physical education. This makes it imperative that students find a placement that is most accurate for them. To assist children, use the following steps. Before doing this activity, students must be able to efficiently place pedometers at their waist.

1. All students place the pedometer at their waist above the knee (see figure 3.2a).

2. Once pedometers are in place, students reset the pedometer and close the face without moving their feet.

3. Instruct students to take 30 steps while counting the number of steps quietly in their head.

4. On the 30th step, they stop and read the pedometer. If the pedometer reads between 27 and 33 steps, they have found an accurate placement.

5. Next, all students, even those who have already found an accurate placement, move the pedometer to the side of the body slightly in front of the hip (see figure 3.2b) and repeat the process described in steps two through four.

Introducing Pedometers to a Class . . .

- The importance of physical activity is often discussed during PE, but how do you know if you are active enough?
- Pedometers are small machines or devices that measure steps and time, depending on the model used.
- Attach it to your waistband or belt directly above the knee. Make sure it is closed.
- Explain the rule "You shake, I take" and why shaking is not a desirable activity.
- Reinforce the importance of honesty, respect, and cooperation when using pedometers, and remind children that using pedometers is a privilege that can be taken away if they don't meet behavior expectations.

After Pedometers Have Been Given to Students . . .

- Allow children to shake the pedometers to observe the numbers increasing and then reset the pedometer.
- Demonstrate appropriate placement and allow students to practice putting the pedometers on correctly.
- Discuss belts for children without a waistband or belt.
- Have youngsters reset the pedometers and walk in the teaching area, periodically checking the pedometer.
- Have the students participate in teacher-directed activities while checking the pedometer from time to time.
- Remind students that step counts and activity time are private and do not have to be shared with peers.
- Explain the distribution and return system and practice by having children retrieve and return the pedometers. This system requires several opportunities for practice before children become efficient with the routine.

Figure 3.1   Instructional points for introducing pedometers.

6. Finally, the same process is done with the pedometer at their waist behind the hip (see figure 3.2c). Students may need the assistance of a partner or teacher to place the pedometer behind them. This position is often an accurate spot for extremely overweight children because there is less body fat and less flexing on the backside.

7. Students should wear the pedometer where they've identified the most accurate reading.

8. At the start of each school year, because of maturation, the process of finding an accurate spot should be revisited to ensure pedometer-count accuracy.

9. These steps can be used with the activity-time function. Have students walk for a set amount of time (e.g., 30 seconds) using each of the three different placements. Start and stop the class and use a stopwatch to monitor the time. The position that yields a time closest to 30 seconds is an accurate placement.

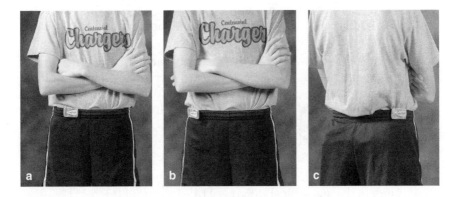

Figure 3.2   Pedometer placement *(a)* above the knee, *(b)* on the side, and *(c)* on the back.

Developing Routines for Pedometer Use

Like with other instructional tasks, students need to learn effective routines to assure efficient use of pedometers. A distribution and return system minimizes disruption and decreases the amount of time necessary for students to acquire and return pedometers. A systematic approach also helps to minimize pedometer loss. The first step in developing pedometer routines is to mark each pedometer with an identification number. An effective and enduring method is to etch numbers on the pedometer. Students are assigned a specific pedometer that they use during physical education class. Because students in other physical education classes are assigned the same pedometers, it is important to have a method for monitoring and storing the pedometers. The system should quickly reveal whether pedometers are missing when it's time to return them. Suggestions for pedometer storage include hanging pocket holders, divided buckets, and a grid shoe holder. If teachers are required to take attendance, this monitoring system can also be used to take attendance: Once students have their pedometers on, pedometers left behind indicate students not in attendance. The following steps are needed for an efficient distribution and return system.

1. Keep a master list of pedometer assignments.
2. Designate a retrieval area for the pedometers. This can be on a stage or around the perimeter of the teaching area. Use the same area each lesson, and place the pedometers in the same sequence to expedite distribution and return.
3. Once students have entered the teaching area, instruct them to get their pedometers and correctly clip them in place. This should be accomplished "on the move" so students are not standing around talking. Students without a belt or waistband should first put on a nylon belt and then fasten the pedometer to it. Ask all students to reset their pedometers to zero after they have fastened them to their waistband.
4. At the conclusion of class, instruct students to return the pedometers to the same location where they acquired them.
5. Before the class leaves, quickly check for missing or damaged pedometers. This check must be done after each class. A student helper or squad leaders can be responsible for checking for missing pedometers. If pedometers are missing or damaged, the master list can be used to identify responsible students.

Monitoring Steps and Minutes of Physical Activity

Using pedometers that measure both steps and minutes of physical activity often leads to the question: Should I monitor steps or physical activity? Although number of steps is certainly a useful and accurate measurement of physical activity, measuring activity time via pedometry is usually a more accurate approach. Activity time is accurate, even at slow walking speeds, as opposed to pedometer step counts, which are often inaccurate at a slow place (Beets, Patton, & Edwards, 2005). Also, activity time eliminates the confounding influence of stride length on pedometer steps. Said another way, people with longer legs and thus, longer strides, take fewer steps than someone with shorter legs to cover the same distance. This concept can lead to misunderstandings and frustration for children. For example, if a tall student and a short student walk together for 30 minutes, the shorter student will accumulate more steps. This can be demoralizing for the taller student. However, when these students examine their activity time, results will be very similar for both students. This same example holds true in physical education classes as well. For these reasons, assessing the activity time of students with a pedometer is usually a more accurate and appropriate measure.

Recording Activity Data

Once students become comfortable wearing pedometers, it is time to start recording their physical activity data. Recording activity data teaches students to monitor their activity patterns over time. Recording physical activity levels exposes students to their physical activity levels and allows them to set personal goals, track their progress (see chapter 4), and determine what types of activities are the most vigorous. Teachers can use data records to evaluate activities and identify students who are at risk of achieving low levels of physical activity.

The following is a list of steps to follow when teaching students to record their daily activity.

1. Develop physical education activity cards. A card can be created for each student or each pedometer. See figure 3.3 for an example.

2. Place an activity card and a pencil with each pedometer. If pedometers are distributed around the perimeter of the teaching area, they can be placed on top of the card. If a hanging holder or shoe organizer is used, the card and a pencil can be placed in the pocket with the pedometer.

3. Students returning pedometers take their data cards, open their pedometers, record their data on the cards, and replace the cards and pedometers. This procedure allows all students to record data privately, without the potential embarrassment of other students seeing their data.

4. Check for missing and damaged pedometers, and, if a card is made for each student, collect the cards from the students. If each student has a separate card, data collection will require teachers to quickly collect the cards from the current class and prepare the cards for the next class. Therefore, implement the data collection procedure one class at a time and become proficient with the procedure before using it with several classes.

Activity Time and Step-Count Log

Name _____ Pedometer # _____ Room # _____

Age _____ Grade _____

	School day		Outside of school	
	Activity time	**Steps**	**Activity time**	**Steps**
Day 1				
Day 2				
Day 3				
Day 4				
Day 5				
Day 6				
Day 7				
Day 8				

Figure 3.3   Example of an eight-day pedometer data card.

Logging Activity Data on the Web

When students begin monitoring their daily activity, it is wise to have them record it on a log sheet as described in the previous section. In addition, they can go to the computer lab and input their data on Web-based monitoring programs. Two of the most popular programs for students and teachers in the United States are described in the following sections.

Presidential Active Lifestyle Award

The President's Council on Physical Fitness and Sports sponsors the Presidential Active Lifestyle Award (PALA). Their Web site (www. presidentschallenge.org) allows students to log their activity time or steps. If they accumulate 60 minutes or 11,000 steps for girls and 13,000 steps for boys for most of the days of the week for six weeks, they can earn the PALA. If 35 percent of the students in a school earn the PALA two or more times during the year, the school can become an Active

Lifestyle Model School. These schools receive a certificate and are recognized on the Web site. The Web site (www.presidentschallenge. org/pdf/pala_activity_log.pdf) offers a brochure explaining the PALA and a log sheet that can be downloaded.

An excellent activity for students is to go to the school computer lab once a week and enter their activity data for the past seven days. If students register on the President's Challenge Web site, they can log on and enter their data directly into the Web site. Student data is stored on the site to help students know when they have met the requirements for the PALA. Students can go to the Web site to register and begin logging in their steps at www.presidentschallenge.org/login/register_individual.aspx.

WalkSmart! Active Schools

WalkSmart! Active Schools is an innovative, Web-based walking program that offers students a motivating way to monitor and increase their daily physical activity—both inside and outside the classroom. It's easy to implement. Teachers can subscribe as a class, an entire school, or a district. A variety of online walks are available, each with its own educational milestones and a dynamic map. If desired, schools can add personalized incentives and prizes to be placed on the educational milestones to provide extra motivation and fun.

In the Walksmart! program, students log steps daily toward an activity goal established at the start of the program. As students log their steps and activity time in the computer lab or at home, they learn about geography, history, and social studies. The following are additional features of the program.

- Each walk includes up to 100 milestones and lasts three to four months.
- Dynamic maps and milestones help students learn as they go.
- Colorful pie charts help students monitor their progress.
- An online journal allows students to write about their experiences.

WalkSmart! Active Schools provides teachers and administrators with valuable feedback on specific outcomes because student data are stored and can be retrieved by teachers and administrators for analysis. It is an innovative way to monitor activity time, steps, and goals by student, class, or grade. Standard reports can be printed to document the impact of the program on overall student activity levels. Parents can also become a part of WalkSmart and participate with their youngsters (www.walksmartactiveschools.com/default_pages/default_home.asp).

Establishing Physical Education Baseline Data

How much activity should students accumulate during a 30-minute lesson? When measuring physical activity in steps, research suggests American students will accumulate between 1,200 and 2,000 steps (Morgan, Pangrazi, & Beighle, 2003; Scruggs et al., 2003; Morgan, Beighle, & Pangrazi, 2005). Only one study has used pedometers to measure the amount of time children spend moving during physical education (Morgan, Beighle, & Pangrazi, 2005). This study found that on average, girls moved for 13 minutes and boys for 17 minutes during a 30-minute lesson. Interestingly, both boys and girls averaged 110 steps per minute over the course of the lesson. Because activity levels will vary from program to program and class to class, it is important to find the average for each class. Initial data collected to determine the average number of steps or minutes students accumulate during physical education are referred to as their *baseline data.* Once teachers know the baseline activity level of individual students and a class, the effectiveness of efforts to improve instruction and increase activity time can be assessed. Specifics on improving instruction are presented in the following section.

To identify the baseline activity levels in your class, do the following:

1. Arrange the pedometers on the stage or around the perimeter of the teaching area with forms that have the students' names and blank spaces for recording the data (see figure 3.3). Or organize students into squads and group the pedometers accordingly.

2. When all the students have their pedometers properly secured, ask them to stand still and reset their pedometers so that everybody starts with zero step counts and zero seconds.

3. Make sure the pedometers remain closed during the entire lesson. Before the end of the class period, have students take their pedometers back to where they picked them up and record their step counts and activity time on the form.

4. Conduct a minimum of four lessons to allow all the students to get an accurate representation of their average lesson activity or baseline data in physical education. Variation exists among different types of lessons. Measuring four different class periods and finding an average score allows for activity differences in lessons.

5. Strategies for using individual baseline data to teach goal setting will be presented in chapter 4.

Improving Instruction With Pedometer Data

What if the data are collected and analyzed and reveal that classes of students are inactive? Does it mean the program is ineffective? No. Does it mean improvements can be made? Yes, all programs can improve. Even if the data reveal that students are adequately active, other ways to further increase their physical activity levels can be found. The following are areas to analyze if increased physical activity is a goal for physical education classes.

Instructional Time

How long are your instructions? Many teachers have a tendency to give lengthy instructions, thus decreasing the amount of activity time. Certainly, it does not make sense to eliminate instruction to increase physical activity time. A better solution is to break up the instruction into 15- to 30-second episodes followed by 60 to 90 seconds of activity or practice time. This approach is much more efficient for young students who are usually able to concentrate on only one or two points at a time.

Management Time

Managing and moving students into instructional formations can take time. Often, it is done with students standing around or counting off, not only inviting discipline problems but also creating a time of inactivity and boredom. Ways to group students include getting them into a circle, having them find partners, or equipping them while keeping them moving and behaving responsibly. Minimizing management time and teaching management skills on the move will increase the amount of activity time and raise the enjoyment level of the lesson (Darst & Pangrazi, 2006; Pangrazi, 2007).

Selection and Modification of Activities

Some types of lessons lend themselves to inactivity. For example, activities organized so that students must wait in line and take turns reduce the amount of activity time. Regularly examining instructional activities to ensure that they offer everyone in the class the maximum amount of participation time will increase the likelihood of students being active and enjoying the experience.

Role Modeling

The ways teachers act and move during physical education classes are important components of effective instruction. Teachers who stand in one place and do not move are likely to have classes that behave in a similar manner. To promote activity among the students, move around the teaching area with vigor and enthusiasm. As the saying goes, "Enthusiasm and moving are contagious . . . spread them."

Lesson Type

Certain lessons in physical education provide less activity than others. Try to find ways to increase activity in low-activity lessons. For instance, some schools require physical education teachers to include health instruction in their lessons. Rather than present a "sit-down" health lesson, use activity as the medium to teach health concepts. Many physical education lessons are much more effective when students can learn on the move.

Environment

Does the environment encourage students to be active? If students are expected to be active and participate in a variety of activities, the physical education environment must be safe and nonthreatening. Students should have opportunities to discover ways to increase the activity in their physical education classes. A simple challenge such as, "Let's see how many different ways you can move while tossing your beanbags," can prompt students to increase their activity levels. Then different students can lead the class in performing their activity ideas.

As just described, many factors affect the amount of physical activity students accumulate in physical education classes. Although pedometer data can be extremely useful, when combined with a videotape of the lesson, these data can be even more powerful.

Implementing Teaching Strategies to Increase Physical Activity

An important strategy for improving instructional effectiveness is to use the baseline data to set instructional goals. Lessons vary in terms of physical activity level. For example, a jogging or walking lesson would undoubtedly result in a higher level of activity than a juggling lesson.

Despite this wide variation, maximizing the number of steps taken in physical education class is a reasonable goal. One way is to alternate low-activity and high-activity instruction. Some data have shown that the majority of U.S. students accumulate only 4,000 steps during the school day (Morgan, Pangrazi, & Beighle, 2003). If 2,000 of those steps are gathered in a 30-minute physical education lesson, it is critical that activity be increased in the sedentary school environment. The following are steps to follow in an effort to increase the activity levels of students.

1. Assuming you have more than one class at each grade level, use this situation to determine how effectively you can modify the physical education environment to ensure adequate activity for your students. Teach one class without modifying the lesson.

2. Change how you teach the second class. Identify an intervention (treatment) that you can implement to increase the amount of activity in your lesson. Here are suggestions:
   □ Add an active game.
   □ Ask the students to walk around the area while they practice skills.
   □ Let students practice with a partner, on the condition that they must be moving.
   □ Add a high-intensity activity such as rope jumping.

3. Gather data on both classes and compare the activity levels. Reflect on the lessons. Did adding more activity increase or reduce the effectiveness of your instruction? Did the students seem more enthusiastic or less enthusiastic about learning? Based on your reflections, determine how this action research can be used in future lessons. The point is to help the students accumulate as much activity as possible. The school environment is primarily a sedentary experience, making an active physical education lesson important.

Final Thoughts

Pedometers add much to the school environment because they offer objective data to students, teachers, and parents about their physical activity level. Establishing procedures for effective use of pedometers will make the experience enjoyable for all. Pedometers offer a relatively inexpensive tool that will help students understand the importance of physical activity and the downside of inactivity.

If You Want to Know More . . .

The following Web sites provide information about pedometers and pedometer accessories in relation to school programs and activities.

Web Sites

www.walk4life.com

This Web site provides a catalog of pedometers, PE teacher kits, pedometer tips, accessories, and more.

www.digiwalker.com

This Web site provides a catalog of pedometers, school kits, and more.

http://activated.det.act.gov.au/hps/tl/feat4feet.htm

This is the Web site for Australia's Feat 4 Feet program.

www.chdf.org.au

This is the Web site for Australia's Centre for Health Promotion.

www.stepscount.com

Step Counts, Inc. is a Web site that provides pedometers, school kits, accessories, and more. It is Canada's top-selling pedometer company.

References

Beets, M.W., Patton, M.M., & Edwards, S. (2005). The accuracy of pedometer steps and time during walking in children. *Medicine and Science in Sports and Exercise, 37*(3), 513-520.

Darst, P. & Pangrazi, R.P. (2006). *Dynamic physical education for secondary school students* (5th ed.). San Francisco: Benjamin Cummings.

Morgan, C.F., Beighle, A., & Pangrazi, R.P. (2005). Does physical education benefit the least active children? *Research Quarterly for Sport and Exercise, 76*(1 Suppl.), A-84.

Morgan, C.F., Pangrazi, R.P., & Beighle, A. (2003). Using pedometers to promote physical activity in physical education. *Journal of Physical Education, Recreation and Dance, 74*(7), 33-38.

Pangrazi, R.P. (2007). *Dynamic physical education for elementary school students* (15th ed.). San Francisco: Benjamin Cummings.

Scruggs, P.W., Beveridge, S.K., Eisenman, P.A., Watson, D.L., Shultz, B.B., & Ransdell, L.B. (2003). Quantifying physical activity via pedometry in elementary physical education. *Medicine and Science in Sports and Exercise, 35*(6), 1065-1071.

Using Pedometers to Teach Self-Management Skills

This chapter presents a variety of pedometer-based self-management skills using pedometers to promote long-term active lifestyles. As with any skill, practicing self-management is essential for success. Therefore, the information and activities in this chapter, along with the pedometer activities in chapters 6 and 7, provide ways to practice self-management skills. Examples of self-management skills (also referred to as self-regulation skills) that are the most pertinent and useful with pedometers include self-assessment, self-monitoring, and goal setting—all skills that can enable people to be successful in their behavior-change efforts (Corbin, Welk, Corbin, & Welk, 2008). Self-assessment and self-monitoring were initially addressed in chapter 3 (obtaining baseline step-count data and recording activity levels) because they are important skills for a healthy lifestyle. Discussion of ways pedometers can be beneficial in teaching other self-management skills such as self-efficacy, motivation, success, social support, and building knowledge are also integrated into the information and activities in this chapter.

The benefit of these particular skills is that they play a role in changing the predisposing, enabling, and reinforcing factors that make it more likely for individuals to adhere to healthy lifestyles (Corbin, Welk, Corbin, & Welk, 2008). Predisposing factors are those that positively influence a person's decision to make a behavior change (e.g., self-efficacy, self-confidence, enjoyment, beliefs, knowledge, and self-motivation). Enabling factors help people carry out a healthy lifestyle plan (e.g., self-planning, self-assessment, self-monitoring, and goal setting), and reinforcing factors encourage people to sustain healthy lifestyles (e.g., social support and success). Although personal factors such as age, gender, and heredity also affect the likelihood of adherence to healthy lifestyles, these are factors that an individual is unable to control. Therefore, physical and health educators must focus on controllable factors to promote long-lasting changes in health behavior.

Self-Efficacy and Motivation

One of the most beneficial and influential predisposing factors for promoting a change in healthy lifestyles is self-efficacy. Self-efficacy is the belief that one has the capabilities to execute the courses of action required to manage prospective situations. For example, if you possess self-efficacy, the belief in your ability to perform a certain task, you are more likely to incorporate that task into your life. More specifically, if you believe you are able to be physically active, meaning you possess self-efficacy for physical activity, you are predisposed to successful adoption of regular physical activity into your life. It is an important challenge for educators to find innovative and effective ways to help students develop self-efficacy to better facilitate their adherence to changes in health behavior. Changing students' belief in their abilities is not an easy task, but one that warrants steadfast pursuit because thoughts lead to action. Lessons that build individual self-confidence and self-esteem through small successes do just that.

Another important predisposing factor for influencing change in health behaviors is motivation. Motivation is the psychological feature that arouses an organism to action toward a goal and gives purpose and direction to the behavior. Figuring out and capitalizing on what gives students a reason or purpose to be healthy and physically active is often the challenge in our sedentary society. Most people do not see the benefit of physical activity or other health behaviors because they are typically more concerned with peer acceptance, immediate gratification, and pleasure, rather than disease prevention and health promotion. This offers a challenge to physical and health educators in this technologically advanced nation of consumerism.

One possible solution to this challenge of motivating students is to remember the acronym PRAISE when teaching (see table 4.1). PRAISE combines two documented theories in the literature: achievement goal theory and self-determination theory (Ntoumanis & Biddle, 1999; Deci & Ryan, 1985), both known to facilitate motivation. Careful consideration of these characteristics in physical education, which means making a concerted effort to create an environment that promotes choice and accomplishment of small tasks (i.e., self-mastery), can lead to increased intrinsic motivation. Being motivated to engage in an activity for the mere joy and satisfaction of the activity itself is considered intrinsic, or self-determined, motivation and is more likely to lead to sustained behavior. PRAISE provides strategies to use in physical education that capitalize on psychological factors related to successful behavior change. Physical educators should be able to turn students on to physical activity, help them assess their physical activity levels, and teach students self-management skills. This involves trying to determine the motivation behind students' behaviors and incorporating PRAISE strategies into lesson planning.

Once students are turned on to physical activity and find success, what will ensure that they maintain their healthy behavior patterns? Enabling factors that were mentioned earlier include goal setting, self-assessment, self-monitoring, and self-planning. Reinforcing factors are a second set that provide support and encouragement to maintain healthy lifestyles. These include experiencing success with the behavior and social support. As depicted by the S in PRAISE, social support can come from family members, peers, teachers, coaches, and other health professionals. It is important to understand that the quantity of social support networks is not as important as the quality of the support. Overall, as educators,

Table 4.1 PRAISE

Concept	Strategies
Perceived competence: a student's belief or opinion of his or her efficacy (ability) in an activity or behavior	• Allow all children to be successful. • Begin with the easiest tasks and progress to the most difficult. • Maximize repetitions and refinement. • Modify activities and games. • Incorporate appropriate activities. • Provide specific, positive feedback, such as "Nice effort. You are working hard and getting lots of activity today." • Emphasize the process of being physically active.
Relatedness: feeling of belongingness and connectedness to others (Ryan & Deci, 2000)	• Get to know students. • Explain why pedometers are being used. • Explain the role of physical activity in lifelong health. • Be an active role model during PE and outside of PE.
Autonomy: sense of choice, volition, and freedom from external pressure toward behaving or thinking a certain way (Ryan & Deci, 2000)	• Promote choice (e.g., have students choose their goals). • Provide several activities from which students can choose within a lesson. • Teach students to assess their own activity levels and set goals.
Individuality: the premise that students have unique needs based on their experiences, heredity, and personal characteristics	• Treat students as individuals. • Teach that physical activity choices are personal. • Explain that different people can have different activity goals. • Treat students fairly and consistently. • Promote individual standards rather than normative standards.
Social support: encouragement, assistance, and role modeling received from parents, teachers, coaches, peers, friends, or other health professionals (Weiss, 2000)	• Understand that peers can influence physical activity choices. • Involve family members when possible. • Be a positive role model. • Start physical activity clubs. • Understand the importance of social groups.
Enjoyment: experiencing satisfaction and pleasure in an activity or behavior	• Use a variety of activities. • Implement a balanced curriculum. • Provide a safe, comfortable, well-managed environment. • Ask students what they enjoy. • Start easy and progress slowly.

employing the use of self-management skills and understanding how and when these factors affect behavior-change efforts are essential for the successful implementation of programs that cultivate long-term healthy lifestyles. The activities presented at the end of this book make use of these self-management skills and demonstrate their importance for developing and implementing effective pedometer lessons.

Because most children are exposed to physical education, this setting provides great potential for teaching self-management skills. Certainly, physical activity programs are not limited to physical education settings. Programs are offered by communities, while others are housed at the state and national levels. Regardless of the setting, pedometers can enhance the effectiveness of an activity program by providing valuable feedback necessary for self-assessment, self-monitoring, and goal setting.

Pedometers and Goal Setting

Goal setting, an important factor, is a self-management skill easily practiced using pedometers. The immediate feedback on physical activity levels provides the user with knowledge and awareness to use when planning a healthy activity program based on personalized goal-setting principles. Taking it one step at a time, literally and figuratively, individuals can assess their activity level and set goals based on their needs, motivation, and commitment.

In the wake of high technology and low activity, it seems imperative that we find ways for people to be more active. Lifestyle activity, or activity that is part of everyday living, such as walking to or from school, taking the stairs, and gardening, has been promoted for 10 years by the Surgeon General of the United States (USDHHS, 1996). Evidence clearly shows that health and wellness gains can result from moderate amounts of this type of activity. Lifestyle activity can be relatively easily incorporated into one's life without having to buy a fitness center membership or exercise equipment, change into "workout clothes," or take a 60-minute block of time out of your day to complete—all factors that often result in lack of adherence to physical activity programs. Pedometers are an excellent tool because they monitor the total volume of lifestyle activity accumulated throughout the day, one step (or stair, or shovel) at a time.

Using pedometers to set specific and realistic activity goals has the potential to change the sedentary environment in which we live. Students can immediately see their progress, make changes when necessary, and be motivated when they achieve their goals. Although goal-setting research originated 30 years ago in the workplace, its use in health promotion has more recently become prevalent. Locke, Shaw, Saari, and Latham (1981,

p. 126) defined a goal as "what an individual is trying to accomplish; it is the object or aim of an action." Applying that to health goals, the "aim of an action" that we strive to achieve is a high quality of life involving healthy behaviors such as physical activity and balanced nutrition. Evidence shows that setting attainable, yet challenging, short-term goals can be helpful, rewarding, and motivating in adhering to active lifestyles. Goal setting provides a strategy for organizing physical activity skills into practical, manageable steps (Shilts, Horowitz, & Townsend, 2004) that leads to favorable outcomes.

Cullen and colleagues provided an example shows how goal setting has been useful in the health field. They developed a four-step goal-setting process for dietitians to use when counseling individuals on how to improve dietary habits (Cullen, Baranowski, & Smith, 2001). These researchers adapted Locke's previous goal-setting research in the workplace to the health-promotion setting by identifying the following four steps (Locke, Shaw, Saari, & Latham, 1981): 1) recognize the need for change, 2) establish a goal, 3) adopt a goal-directed activity and self-monitor it, and 4) self-reward goal attainment (see figure 4.1). The first step in recognizing the need for change can be likened to self-assessment.

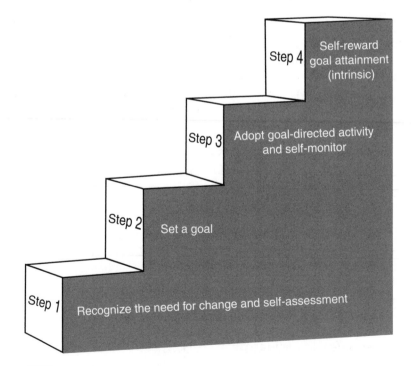

Figure 4.1   Steps to successful goal setting.

The second step of establishing a goal is obviously goal setting. The third step involves self-monitoring the goal-directed activity. Lastly, the fourth step contributes to the motivation necessary to initiate a life change, with the hope that such rewards are based on pursuing the goal for the joy and satisfaction of the behavior itself. Although additional goal-setting research with adolescents and children in nutrition and physical activity programs is needed, these goal-setting principles based on sound theory can be effectively used in physical education, community health promotion, and even within the family unit.

With the advent of accurate and reliable digital pedometers over the last 10 years and the U.S. Surgeon General's lifestyle activity recommendations, setting goals has become more common. Unfortunately, goals are often established without concern for the needs of a specific age group and fail to follow theory-driven practices. For example, it is not an acceptable practice to set a daily 10,000-step goal simply because it has been espoused many times in the press. To be useful and effective, researchers agree that the goals must be appropriate for the specific age group with whom you are working. Locke and his colleagues found that proximal, specific, difficult, yet realistic goals resulted in higher task performance compared to no goal or easily attained goals (Locke, Shaw, Saari, & Latham, 1981). This implies that the most effective goals are short term, explicit, and somewhat challenging in nature, thus requiring effort for achievement and a resulting sense of accomplishment. If goals are too easily reached, they are less likely to be effective in creating long-lasting behavior change. That being said, physical activity outcomes should address three characteristics of a goal: 1) its properties, which are proximity, specificity, and difficulty; 2) its components, which are feedback and rewards; and 3) its type, which are self-set, assigned or prescribed, participatory and collaborative, or guided (a new goal-setting strategy). Researchers have concluded that optimal manipulation of these characteristics based on individual needs is vital to motivation, self-efficacy, and behavior change in adults (Shilts, Horowitz, & Townsend, 2004).

The nature of pedometer step-count feedback is specific, so the short-term, difficult, yet attainable, aspects can be individually manipulated based on an individual's personal activity level and goals. For instance, establishing a baseline step count, then deciding the amount of time necessary to achieve a higher step count can vary depending on the person and his or her current physical activity level, time commitment, and overall situation. Suitable goals that take these factors into consideration might be to increase step counts or activity time by 10 percent or to increase steps per minute. These increases can apply to daily or weekly goals. For example, instead of saying "I would like to be more active," a more appropriate and effective goal would be this: "With my baseline step count of 2,500 steps and activity time of 32 minutes, I would like to increase my step count to 2,750 and activity time to 36 minutes each day for the next four weeks and then reevaluate." For further examples that provide tangible ways for you to adapt different goal-setting techniques to your particular setting and situation, refer to the goal-setting activities presented in the following section and in chapters 5, 6, and 7. It is important to emphasize that the first step in achieving a goal is the belief in one's ability to achieve that goal (self-efficacy).

Setting Individual Activity Goals

Pedometers are an excellent tool for teaching students how to set activity goals in physical education. When students learn to monitor their daily activity levels and set goals, they are accepting the responsibility for accumulating adequate daily activity. Setting goals is not a competitive endeavor; rather, it is a unique and personal matter. This type of goal setting is another way of illustrating the importance of the I for individuality and the A for autonomy in the PRAISE acronym. The desired outcome for activity goals is for each student to become aware of how active he or she is and how active he or she needs to be for good health. Then students can modify their daily activity based on pedometer data rather than a general guess. The following is a lesson designed to teach students about goal setting:

Expected Outcomes

- To teach students how to set personal activity goals based on pedometer step counts
- To learn to log daily physical activity
- To teach students to chart their data in a spreadsheet

Equipment and Setting

One pedometer per student

General Instructions

1. Have students secure a pedometer. Students clear their pedometer and start their step count as soon as they are ready for class participation.
2. Design a personal-goal card (see Setting Personal Activity Goals With Pedometers on page 59) that allows students to log the step counts of the activities they are doing and what their personal goal is.
3. Gather three to four weeks of physical education class activity so students can see whether they are reaching their personal goals.

Setting Personal Activity Goals With Pedometers

Your goal should be based on how active you are most days. Do not compare your performance with others because everyone has different responsibilities.

The first thing you have to do is find your baseline activity level.

Calculate Your Baseline Step Counts

Elementary school students	Middle and high school students
Day 1 step counts _____ Day 2 step counts _____ Day 3 step counts _____ Day 4 step counts _____ Total step counts _____ divided by 4 equals _____. This number is your **baseline activity** and will be used to determine your personal activity goal.	Day 1 step counts _____ Day 2 step counts _____ Day 3 step counts _____ Day 4 step counts _____ Day 5 step counts _____ Day 6 step counts _____ Day 7 step counts _____ Day 8 step counts _____ Total step counts _____ divided by 8 equals _____. This number is your **baseline activity** and will be used to determine your personal activity goal.

Next, calculate your personal step-count goal as shown in the examples.

Calculate Your Step-Count Goal

Baseline	Personal goal (10% of your baseline plus your baseline)	Weeks	Total step counts
4,000 steps	$4{,}000 \times 0.10 + 4{,}000$	1 and 2	4,400
	Every two weeks thereafter, the goal will be increased by 400 steps.	3 and 4	4,800
		5 and 6	5,200
		7 and 8	5,600
		9 and 10	6,000
6,000 steps	$6{,}000 \times 0.10 + 6{,}000$	1 and 2	6,600
	Every two weeks thereafter, the goal will be increased by 600 steps.	3 and 4	7,200
		5 and 6	7,800
		7 and 8	8,400
		9 and 10	9,000

From Robert P. Pangrazi, Aaron Beighle, and Cara L. Sidman, 2007, *Pedometer Power, Second Edition*, (Champaign, IL: Human Kinetics).

4. When possible, after several days of recording physical education class activity in their logs, have students chart their data in Excel during a computer class.

5. Review the data by asking questions such as these:

   □ Did your step counts change because of different types of activities?

   □ What is a reasonable goal? How many steps should you try to increase each week (5 to 10 percent)?

   □ How could you accumulate more steps in physical education class or during free time?

Teaching Hints

With the cooperation of the classroom teacher, have students wear the pedometers during the entire school day and record step counts.

Creating Cooperative Class Goals

Goal setting can also be used as a project for the entire class and can facilitate social support, an important factor in reinforcing a behavior. The goal-setting process is similar to the one used to set individual goals, except that the whole class works together for a common goal. This common goal-setting technique includes all students and helps to establish cooperative goals and a sense that everybody belongs in the group.

Expected Outcomes

- To teach children to set group goals
- To teach cooperation and relatedness with the entire class
- To teach children to encourage and support others in the class
- To teach children to think about ways to increase physical activity

Equipment and Setting

One pedometer per student

General Instructions

1. For one week, have children record their physical education step counts each day.

2. At the end of the week, the number of steps accumulated during physical education classes by all students is added into a single total.

3. On the first physical education class of the following week, tell the class their total number of step counts. Involve the class in determining what their class goal for the coming week will be.

4. If the class reaches their selected goal, a new discussion is conducted to establish a new level. If the goal is not reached, the goal is maintained and discussions can cover how to increase their physical activity levels.

Variations

- This activity can be performed with small groups of students during physical education classes.

- Goals can also be set for a 15-minute increment during one physical education lesson.

- Students can wear the pedometers during school for the entire week. The class can estimate or guess how many steps they will accumulate during school. This often fosters discussions regarding how to increase daily physical activity levels.

- Step counts can be converted into miles or kilometers and related to a similar distance in the area (e.g., from Main Street to the elementary school).

Teaching Hints

- Individual student data should never be disclosed without the child's permission. Similarly, children should never be forced to reveal their step counts, either to a teacher, another student, or on a card.

- If only pedometer ID numbers are used to identify students, teachers can designate children to add the accumulated steps. Avoid asking students to calculate the data of other students when their names are visible.

- If the class does not reach their goal, discuss why or why not. Explain that some physical education lessons may be more active than others (e.g., rhythms vs. softball).

- All students should be encouraged to be positive and to be supportive of their classmates. Negative comments regarding step counts constitute unacceptable behavior.

Setting Step Goals for Discretionary-Time Activity

Even though the school day is structured with most time spent in a sedentary setting, discretionary time is available for students. The most obvious times available are before and after school and during recess and the lunch hour. These discretionary times are unique opportunities to increase the overall activity levels of students. Pedometers can be used to show how easy it is to increase physical activity during free periods in school.

Expected Outcomes

- To teach students about their activity levels during free time
- To increase the number of steps students accumulate during their discretionary time

Equipment and Setting

One pedometer per student

General Instructions

1. Perform this activity with one class per week. Take one class for the week (assuming there is only one set of pedometers available).

2. Prepare the pedometers and record cards (see Increasing Physical Activity During Discretionary Time on page 63) for use in homeroom class the first thing each morning. Upon arrival at school, students put the pedometer on and wear it throughout the day. Say nothing to students about the pedometers other than that they will be used to gather activity data and all they have to do is wear the pedometer. Gather two days of data without discussion. Students record their steps on the record card at the end of the day and turn them in to the homeroom teacher.

3. After two days of data gathering, discuss the baseline data with the students. Introduce an intervention plan by asking each student to try to increase the number of steps they accumulated by 10 percent over the next two days. Emphasis should be on encouraging students to select activities they enjoy. Try some of the following intervention strategies for free time periods:

   □ No standing or sitting during recess and noon-hour free times. Be involved in a game, walking and talking with a friend, or practicing a physical skill such as rope jumping, shooting baskets, or dribbling a soccer ball.

   □ Take a walk with a friend.

   □ Play hopscotch or Frisbee golf.

4. Record the step counts for each day of intervention. Again, chart the data and compare the first two days of activity to the second two days. Discuss how more steps are accumulated when people make active choices and select activities they like to do.

5. Move the pedometers to a new class and repeat the entire process.

Increasing Physical Activity During Discretionary Time

Name _____ Class _____ Pedometer # _____

Activity	Steps accumulated	Date
Preintervention steps accumulated		
Day 1		
Day 2		
Postintervention steps accumulated		
Day 3		
Day 4		

From Robert P. Pangrazi, Aaron Beighle, and Cara L. Sidman, 2007, *Pedometer Power, Second Edition,* (Champaign, IL: Human Kinetics).

Calculating Stride Length

At times it is interesting to know how far you have walked rather than how many steps you have taken. In fact, you may want to calculate the distance you walked in one day so you can estimate how far you have hiked or jogged, and use this method to provide variety in goal setting. Two of the easiest ways to measure stride length (the distance you cover with one step) are described here.

Expected Outcome

To learn how to measure stride length

Equipment and Setting

- One pedometer per student
- Marked distance of 30 feet (9 meters)
- Cones to mark starting and finish lines
- Puddle or bucket of water and dry pavement

Thirty-Foot Walk

Use the following steps to easily calculate stride length.

1. Set up a stride-length measurement station by placing two lines 30 feet (9 meters) apart. Mark the starting and end points with cones so it is easy for students to see the station points. If you are in a gymnasium, the width of a volleyball court is 29 feet, 6 inches. Add another six inches (15 centimeters) and you have an easy way to find 30 feet (9 meters).

2. Instruct students to count the number of steps it takes them to travel between the lines. Students start 10 to 15 feet (3 to 4.5 meters) behind the starting line and walk toward the line at a normal pace. Students count their first step as the one that touches the ground inside the starting line. Students continue walking and counting steps until a foot touches outside the finish line. That is the number of steps they will use to calculate their stride length.

3. Students record the number of steps it took to cover the distance.

4. Use table 4.2 to find stride length.

Wet-Foot Walk

Another way to measure stride length is to walk through a water puddle onto dry pavement and measure the distance from heel to heel of the wet footprints. The key is to measure heel to heel or from toe to toe, not from one heel to the other toe.

Table 4.2   Calculating Stride Length

Number of steps over a 30-foot (9-m) distance	Stride length in feet and inches	Stride length in centimeters
8	3'9"	112
9	3'4"	100
10	3'0"	90
11	2'9"	82
12	2'6"	75
13	2'4"	69
14	2'2"	64
15	2'0"	60
16	1'11"	56
17	1'9"	53
18	1'8"	50
19	1'7"	47
20	1'6"	45

Converting Steps to Mileage

 Many students want to know the distance they have walked. Once students understand how far they are walking, it is easier to compare different walks, to understand how long it will take to hike trails and routes, and to better understand their distance for other goal-setting options. With practice, students can learn to convert steps to miles or kilometers with little trouble.

Expected Outcome

To calculate total distance covered

Equipment and Setting

- One pedometer per student
- Marked distance of 100 feet (30.5 meters)

General Instructions

1. Students determine the length of their stride (in feet or in centimeters). It is easiest to use decimals and calculate it as 2.15, 2.75 feet (65.5, 84 centimeters), and so on.

2. Multiply the number of accumulated steps by stride length. For example, if a student has walked 1,200 steps, multiply that number by his or her stride length. Assume her stride length is 2.75 feet (84 centimeters) multiplied by 1,200 steps. The distance walked equals 3,300 feet (100,800 centimeters, or 1,008 meters).

3. Convert feet to mileage by dividing 5,280 (the number of feet in a mile) into the number of feet walked. In this example, 3,300 divided by 5,280 equals 0.625 mile. If you use the metric system, convert meters to kilometers. In this case, it would be 1.008 kilometers, or, when rounded off, 1 kilometer.

Integrating Self-Management Skills

With the increased pressure on students to perform well on standardized tests, many physical education teachers are asked to integrate academic subject matter into their curriculum. Working closely with classroom teachers can create goodwill and positive feelings toward physical education. It also exposes classroom teachers to physical education that they may not receive otherwise. Using pedometers in the school setting provides many opportunities to integrate several subject areas into physical education. It can also help students build knowledge, another important self-management skill predisposing them to success- ful behavior change.

Integration requires working closely with classroom teachers and other special teachers. Accumulating files of topics and specific information taught in the classroom is helpful. As pedometers become part of the curriculum, physical education teachers and classroom teachers can brainstorm and generate ideas regarding ways to integrate pedometers and self-management skills into the classroom with minimal disruption. Many ideas for integrating pedometer data into other academic areas are presented in the following chapters. All of these ideas are marked with this symbol: . The following are brief examples of how to integrate pedometers into other subject areas.

- Learn about hypothesis testing in science by asking students to create a hypothesis that states how active they are during physical educa- tion classes. Students then monitor and log their step data, test the hypothesis, and write a short discussion about their experiment.

- Using the same data, have students enter the data in a spreadsheet and generate a graph of their activity level over several physical education classes. The assignment is completed by asking students to write a paper interpreting the graphed data.

- To use math, history, and geography skills, teach students to calculate the distance they walk in one month in their physical education class, then ask them to choose a historically significant point that distance from home, map their route, and write a brief report on it.

Writing Prompts for Classroom Teachers

Another way to build students' knowledge of the importance of physical activity for long-term health is through relevant writing prompts, which are something for which classroom teachers are continually searching. The following topics provide valid and compelling issues for students who have had experiences with pedometer use. The three types of writing—narrative, expository, and persuasive—can be incorporated to serve both classroom teacher and physical education specialist. The following cross-curriculum integration can be implemented to demonstrate a student's knowledge of the role of physical activity in long-term health and thus provide assessment for physical education specialists. At the same time, classroom teachers may draw on actual experiences derived by all students in their PE classes and use this to demonstrate writing skills. Possible prompts are suggested below:

- **Narrative:** Write a paper describing your days spent wearing a pedometer and monitoring your step counts. What did the pedometer tell you about yourself? How do you feel about what you learned? What types of things did you do during those days, and what things do you think were best for your health? Do you do things that are not good for you? (Narrative writing tells about an event, describes feelings, and provides reactions.)
- **Expository:** Write a paper that explains to someone why a person wears a pedometer and how to wear a pedometer. Things such as how to put it on and when to wear it would be important. You could explain what a pedometer measures or tells you and why this information is important. (Expository writing explains something or describes how to do something. Directions and reports should be given without feeling.)
- **Persuasive:** Write a paper that persuades people to wear a pedometer. Why should they wear one and what will it do for them? Why do you think it is important and what benefits will it provide? (Persuasive writing takes a side and then attempts to convince or persuade someone to that side by providing reasons.)

Final Thoughts

Although physical education is the most common place to practice self-management skills using pedometers, programs in other settings are used throughout the country. For example, the state of Arizona uses the Promoting Lifestyle Activity for Youth (Pangrazi, Beighle, Vehige, & Vack, 2003) program in many of its schools. This program, sponsored by the Arizona Department of Health Services, incorporates activity breaks into the school day that are conducted by the classroom teacher. Pedometers are now used in the program to promote student and family activity and to assess the effectiveness of the program. The book, *Active Youth* (Sammann, 1998), describes the PLAY program and other exemplary programs that work in meeting the Centers for Disease Control and Prevention guidelines.

Regardless of where the program is implemented or by whom, using pedometers provides a useful method for setting goals for physical activity and for assessing, monitoring, planning, and promoting physical activity. Using them in physical education programs to teach self-management skills is fundamental to educators' efforts to increase the activity levels of children. There is no limit to the creative use of pedometers in physical education and other settings as long as their use is based on enhancing self-efficacy, increasing intrinsic motivation, promoting success and social support, and building knowledge to facilitate a lifetime of healthy behaviors. Additional pedometer activities facilitating these critical self-management skills can be found in chapters 5, 6, and 7.

If You Want to Know More . . .

The Web sites that follow offer both practical and research information about the wide range of ways to use pedometers.

Web Sites

www.aahperd.org

This is the site for the American Alliance for Health, Physical Education, Recreation and Dance.

www.aahperd.org/naspe/template.cfm

This site is for the National Association for Sport and Physical Education.

www.indiana.edu/~preschal/

This President's Challenge site is for the physical activity and fitness awards program advocated by the President's Council on Physical Fitness and Sports.

http://pecentral.org

PE Central is a comprehensive Web site for health and physical education teachers that includes a wide range of activities, including pedometer lessons.

www.achper.org.au

This is the site of the Australian Council for Health, Physical Education and Recreation.

www.ausport.gov.au/schools/index.asp

Active Australia Schools Network is a site that supports schools that value sport and physical activity.

www.cahperd.ca

This is the site for the Canadian Association for Health, Physical Education, Recreation and Dance.

www.lin.ca

The Canadian Lifestyle Information Network offers information exchange for organizations and practitioners.

www.afpe.org.uk/

This site is for the Association for Physical Education in the United Kingdom.

References

Corbin, C.B., Welk, G.J., Corbin, W.R., & Welk, K.A. (2008). *Concepts of fitness and wellness: A comprehensive lifestyle approach* (7th ed.). Boston: McGraw-Hill.

Cullen, K.W., Baranowski, T., & Smith, S.P. (2001). Using goal setting as a strategy for dietary behavior change. *Journal of the American Medical Association, 101,* 562-566.

Deci, E.L. & Ryan, R.M. (1985). *Intrinsic motivation and self-determination in human behavior.* New York: Plenum.

Lee, T.W., Locke, E.A., & Latham, G.P. (1989). Goal setting theory and job performance. In: L. Pervin (Ed.), *Goal Concepts in Personality and Social Psychology.* Hillsdale, NJ: Lawrence Erlbaum.

Locke, E.A., Shaw, K.N., Saari, L.M., & Latham, G.P. (1981). Goal setting and task performance: 1969-1980. *Psychological Bulletin, 90,* 125-152.

Ntoumanis, N. & Biddle, S.J.H. (1999). A review of psychological climate in physical activity settings with particular reference to motivation. *Journal of Sport Sciences, 17,* 643-665.

Pangrazi, R.P., Beighle, A., Vehige, T., & Vack, C. (2003). Impact of promoting lifestyle activity for youth (PLAY) on children's physical activity. *Journal of School Health, 73*(8), 317-321.

President's Council on Physical Fitness and Sports. (2006). *The President's Challenge Physical Activity and Fitness Awards Program.* Bloomington, IN: The President's Challenge.

Ryan, R.M. & Deci, E.L. (2000). Self-determination theory and the facilitation of intrinsic motivation, social development, and well-being. *American Psychologist, 55*(1), 68-78.

Sammann, P. 1998. *Active youth: Ideas for implementing CDC physical activity promotion guidelines.* Champaign, IL: Human Kinetics.

Shilts, M.K., Horowitz, M., & Townsend, M.S. (2004). Goal setting as a strategy for dietary and physical activity behavior change: A review of the literature. *American Journal of Health Promotion, 19*(2), 81-93.

U.S. Department of Health and Human Services. (1996). *Physical activity and health: A report of the Surgeon General.* U.S. Department of Health and Human Services, Centers for Disease Control and Prevention, and National Center for Chronic Disease Prevention and Health Promotion. (Eds.). Atlanta: Author.

Weiss, M.R. (2000). Motivating kids in physical activity. *PCPFS Research Digest, 3*(11), 1-8.

Activities for Elementary School Students

Activities in this chapter teach students how pedometers work, expose them to using pedometers as a tool for monitoring physical activity, and help teachers promote physical activity in their physical education programs. The ideas in this chapter assume a basic understanding of pedometer use. Even though these activities have been designated for elementary school students, they can be used as introductory activities for students of any age.

Learning About Steps and Activity Time

Pedometers measure steps and activity time. This activity helps students understand how the devices do that and is particularly useful as an introduction. However, it can be used during any pedometer lesson.

Expected Outcomes

- To expose students to pedometers
- To make students aware of how much activity they accumulate

Equipment and Setting

- One pedometer per student
- Optional equipment as desired by teacher

General Instructions

1. The activity begins with all students in scattered formation.
2. The teacher gives students a series of challenges.
   - How many steps can you accumulate in 30 seconds?
   - How many steps can you accumulate in one minute while moving around the gym touching different lines?
   - How many steps can you take in a 30-second game of tag?
   - How many seconds of activity are recorded in a 45-second game of tag?
   - How many seconds of activity can you accumulate while playing catch with your partner for one minute?
   - How many steps do you take in one minute of jumping jacks? Does one jumping jack equal one step?
3. Once the routine and activity are established, spread challenges throughout the lesson.

10 Steps

A creative way for students to learn how pedometers record step counts is to perform different movements for the same number of steps. In the following activity, different movements are performed exactly 10 times to determine if there is any variation in the number of steps recorded.

Expected Outcome

To determine the step count of various physical activities that have different movement patterns

Equipment and Setting

- One pedometer per student
- Space to move (can be inside or outside)

General Instructions

1. Reset the pedometer to zero before each activity.
2. Perform each of the activities exactly 10 times and record the step count in the appropriate column in the Comparing Step Counts for Different Movements worksheet on page 75.
3. Discuss possible reasons that the pedometer step count was exactly 10, was higher, or was lower and provide comments.

Estimating Steps and Time

This lesson helps students learn to estimate the number of steps and amount of time it takes to cover a specific distance. This activity affords itself to integrating math concepts such as measuring and estimating.

Expected Outcomes

- To teach students to estimate steps and activity time
- To teach students to estimate distance

Equipment and Setting

One pedometer per student

General Instructions

1. Students prepare for the activity by standing on a line on one side of the teaching area.
2. Each student estimates how many steps it will take to walk across the teaching area to another line or landmark. Remind students to keep their estimate to themselves and not say it out loud.

3. Next, repeat the activity by asking students to make another guess and walk the same distance back to the starting point.

4. Have students walk another distance and guess the steps. After a few trials, students' skill in estimating steps and time will start to improve.

5. Finally, if pedometers that measure activity time are available, follow steps 2 through 4, using time as the measure. Remind students to walk at a comfortable pace and guess the time it will take to walk that distance.

Guess and Check

Another method of teaching students about physical activity is to help them understand the difference between active and inactive. Guess and Check encourages students to evaluate the activity they accumulate in a physical education lesson. This activity sharpens estimation skills.

Expected Outcomes

- To teach students the difference between *active* and *inactive*
- To teach students how to estimate step counts
- To allow students to estimate their own activity by measuring step counts or activity time or both and check the accuracy of their predictions

Equipment and Setting

One pedometer per student

General Instructions

1. Have students wear pedometers during several physical education lessons and ask them to make periodic checks of their step counts or activity time. These values indicate how many steps students take and how much time they spend moving during physical education class.

2. Introduce a variety of lessons that produce a wide range of step counts and activity time. For example, a gymnastics lesson usually produces fewer steps than a basketball lesson.

3. Explain to the class the focus of the lesson and ask them to guess the amount of activity they will accumulate during the first half of the class.

4. Halfway through the lesson, have students check their pedometer to see how close their estimates were. Ask them to reset the pedometers and make another guess based on the description of the activities for the remainder of class.

Comparing Step Counts for Different Movements

	Activity	Pedometer step count	Possible reasons for step count
1	Jump		
2	Baby steps		
3	Giant steps		
4	Hops		
5	Slides		
6	Gallops		
7	Fast walk		
8	Slow walk		
9	Backward walk		
10	Jumping jacks		
11	Twists		
12	Skips		
13	Crunches		
14	Other?		

From Robert P. Pangrazi, Aaron Beighle, and Cara L. Sidman, 2007, *Pedometer Power, Second Edition*, (Champaign, IL: Human Kinetics).

5. At the end of class, have students check their pedometers again to see how accurate their prediction was for the second half of class.

6. At the end of class, discuss why their estimates were accurate or inaccurate. Emphasize that estimation is a skill that takes practice and that they will improve as they start to understand which activities are the most active or inactive.

7. Repeat the procedure with a variety of lessons. Each time you discuss the guesses, tie in previous lessons. Prompt the class with questions such as, "Was gymnastics more active than basketball? Why or why not?"

Teaching Hints

- Students should learn to accurately predict the amount of activity they will accumulate during an entire lesson depending on the type of lesson it is.

- If you incorporate a fitness component into the lesson, let students guess and check their steps during the fitness portion.

- Discuss the limitations of pedometers (e.g., pedometers only measure locomotor movement and not stationary activities such as strength exercises or stretches). Ask the question, "If a pedometer can't measure an activity, does that mean it is not beneficial?"

No Steps

When introduced to pedometers, students want to know how they work. Students need to know that the pedometer must be vertical to count the up-and-down movement of the body. No Steps helps students learn which types of movements pedometers cannot count accurately.

Expected Outcomes

- To learn proper pedometer placement
- To explore the types of activities pedometers do not count accurately

Equipment and Setting

One pedometer per student

General Instructions

1. While wearing a pedometer, all students line up on one side of the teaching area.

2. Challenge students to move to the other side of the teaching area without accumulating steps on their pedometer.

3. Once students reach the other side, they should immediately open their pedometer and check to see if step counts were recorded. Challenge them to try to create another way of moving without accumulating steps.

Teaching Hints

- Some students will immediately think to leave the pedometer open. This is an excellent strategy and demonstrates that they understand that the pedometer will not work with the cover open.

- Students may also take the pedometer off. This too shows that they understand how pedometers work.

- Explain that they cannot use either of the previously stated methods but instead must see if they can find ways to move that do not accumulate step counts on the pedometer.

Design a Route

Several programs exist that you can coordinate with pedometer step-count lessons. For example, the Centers for Disease Control and Prevention advocates a walk-to-school program for students (see the Web site www. cdc.gov/nccdphp/dnpa/kidswalk). Teaching students how to choose safe routes with less traffic and fewer busy streets to cross is an important outcome of this activity.

Expected Outcomes

- To provide students the opportunity to design walking and jogging routes on and off school grounds

- To add variety to a walking and jogging lesson

- To encourage students to cooperate with classmates

Equipment and Setting

- One pedometer per student

- One map of the school grounds and neighborhood for each group

- Pencils for recording data

General Instructions

1. Draw maps of the school area and the surrounding neighborhood and mark locations that are off-limits for students.

2. At the beginning of the lesson, discuss the importance of walking and jogging in promoting health and fitness. Explain the importance of pace and walking with a friend. Discuss safety issues such as avoiding streets with high levels of traffic, not talking to strangers, and walking where other students and parents walk.

3. Organize students into groups of three or four. Ask each student to wear a pedometer.

4. Give each group a map of the school grounds. After they learn the school area, students can make maps of their neighborhood.

5. Record the number of steps and activity time students needed to walk their selected routes. Calculate the total score by adding the scores of all students in the group. Mark the legend for the map in steps.

Teaching Hints

- Allow groups to switch maps and walk routes planned by their peers.
- Before they start the walk, ask students to guess how many steps or how much time the route will require.
- Let students use routes from other classes and see if their group accumulates the same number of steps or minutes of activity. Discuss why or why not.

Classroom Integration

Ask students to spell their name or spelling-lesson words, make shapes, or draw pictures with their steps and see how many steps their name requires. Also, reinforce terms from academic areas, such as *perimeter* and *diagonal.*

Graphing Step Counts

 Once students have collected step counts for a few days or more, teach them to chart and graph them. The graphs give students a visual representation of their physical activity. Graphing step counts is an opportunity to work with a computer or math teacher. Students can record their step counts and enter the data on simple electronic spreadsheets and graph the data in a variety of ways. Graphing manually with paper and pencil is also an option.

Expected Outcomes

- To teach students to produce a graph of their step counts for a given amount of time
- To integrate physical activity and physical education into academic areas

Equipment and Setting

- One graphing sheet per student (see the step count data sheet on page 80)
- One pencil per student

General Instructions

1. Produce a graph of the students' step counts for a given amount of time.
2. Ask students to identify ways they can increase their physical activity. List the top five suggestions and test them to see if they are effective.
3. Ask students to analyze the graph and write a brief discussion of their activity level. For example, a student might discuss why he or she was very active one day and relatively inactive the next.

Classroom Integration

- Intermediate-grade students can use step-count data and graphs to calculate means and predict future activity levels. Students can brainstorm to determine why they reached different levels of activity. Ask them to write short essays about their physical activity level based on the graphed data.
- Guessing and making predictions based on the graph is an introduction to the scientific method. Have students develop questions and hypotheses related to physical activity and step counts.

Understanding Individual Differences

It is well established that wide differences exist among students and their ability to perform physical fitness activities. One way to help students understand these differences is to use pedometers so students can measure how many steps they accumulate in an exercise setting. They will learn that their peers accumulate more or fewer steps than they do and that they need to respect these differences.

Expected Outcomes

- To monitor the level of activity each student accumulates in a fitness activity
- To offer students a chance to control the number of steps they accumulate during fitness activities
- To encourage social support during physical activity

Gathering Data and Graphing the Data

Name _____ Teacher _____ Pedometer # _____

	PE activity	Steps	Minutes	Date
Day 1				
Day 2				
Day 3				
Day 4				
Day 5				
Day 6				
Day 7				
Day 8				

My Step Graph

·	Day 1	Day 2	Day 3	Day 4	Day 5	Day 6	Day 7	Day 8
2,000								
1,800								
1,600								
1,400								
1,200								
1,000								
800								
600								
400								
200								
0								

Why do you think you were more active in some lessons than in others?

_____

_____

_____

From Robert P. Pangrazi, Aaron Beighle, and Cara L. Sidman, 2007, *Pedometer Power, Second Edition*, (Champaign, IL: Human Kinetics).

Equipment and Setting

- One pedometer per student
- Equipment for fitness activities

General Instructions

1. Design a fitness routine that alternates aerobic exercises with strength and flexibility exercises.
2. Ask students to find a workout partner and give each pair the following challenge: accumulate 1,200 steps as a team. While one person does a strength or flexibility exercise, the other person does aerobic walking, running in place, or any other form of aerobic exercise for 30 to 60 seconds.
3. Have students switch exercise roles after 30 to 60 seconds and continue until the 1,200 steps are accumulated.

The goal is to teach students to work together while learning that fitness is personal. In some pairs, one partner may accumulate 700 steps, whereas the other accumulates 500 steps. Teach them to record the steps performed during each interval and to total the number of accumulated steps.

Pedometer Orienteering

Orienteering is growing in popularity throughout the world. It combines hiking and walking with using a compass to find directions. Adding pedometers to orienteering can help students learn to estimate various distances and the number of steps required to cover those distances. This activity uses visual sightings instead of compasses; however, you can use compasses if they are available.

Expected Outcomes

- To expose students to the lifestyle activity of orienteering
- To teach students to find geographic coordinates using a compass
- To teach students to estimate distances and read compass directions

Equipment and Setting

- Map of school grounds (see figure 5.1 for an example)
- Direction sheet for each landmark
- Clipboard and pencil for each group
- Hoops and cones to mark landmarks
- Compasses (optional)

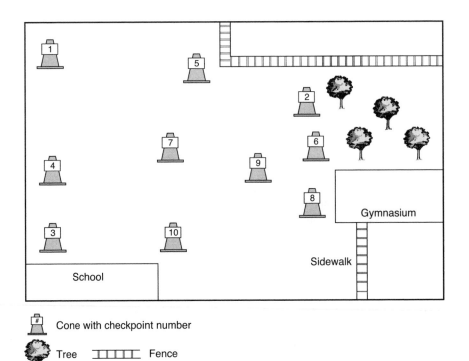

Figure 5.1   Sample orienteering course.

General Instructions

1. Design an orienteering course using different landmarks for visual sightings. Allow students to work in small groups. Create enough markers that each group can start at a different marker. Each marker should have directions that include visual sighting directions and distance in steps to the next marker.

2. Once the sighting is made, students walk the designated number of steps (directions should include a range of steps to accommodate different stride lengths) in that direction to a hoop. Students then refer to their direction sheet, which gives them a new visual sighting landmark and number of steps to travel. The goal is to reach all the hoops.

3. As students navigate the course, move around the course and offer them feedback and support if they become confused.

Teaching Hints

■ Figure 5.1 shows a sample course using the school and playground area. Students can start at any point on the course.

- Activities can be made more difficult by putting directions to the next station at each checkpoint. This way, if students do not find the stations, they will not be able to complete the course.

- Also, instead of using visual sighting, direct students by compass bearings and steps (for example, "From the monkey bars, take a compass bearing of 200 degrees and walk 325 steps").

- Figure 5.2 shows sample directions for a beginning course and an intermediate course that incorporate bearings. The letters listed in figure 5.2*a* are used in the Pedometer Scavenger Hunt on page 87.

Classroom Integration

Before starting this activity, discuss compass points (north, south, east, and west) with students. Explain how compasses work and how to use the sun to determine direction. Mark the perimeter walls of the gym and school with N, S, E, and W.

Checkpoint	Landmark	Number of steps	Letter
1	Monkey bars	175-200	A
2	Flagpole	60-85	Y
3	Parking lot gate	250-275	I
4	Front door of gym	150-175	T
5	Door of room 9	100-125	C
6	Drinking fountain	300-325	V
7	Basketball court	160-185	T
8	Trash can by principal's office	125-150	I

a

Take 125 steps NE toward marker 5.

Proceed 85 steps S around the slide to marker 2.

Walk backward in a SW direction for 110 steps to marker 1.

Jog 75 steps N to marker 3.

Skip SW 140 steps to marker 4.

Take 75 steps NE toward the slide. From this point, jog 25 steps W to marker 6.

Slide 45 times NW toward marker 8.

Marker 7 is 85 steps SE of marker 8.

b

Figure 5.2   Samples of orienteering directions. *(a)* Beginner course with visual landmarks. *(b)* Intermediate course with directions.

Pedometer Frisbee Golf

Frisbee golf is similar to regular golf, except that Frisbee throws count as strokes. Pedometers give the game a different twist. In this variation, students play regular Frisbee golf; however, scorekeeping rules are different. High and low individual step counts and high and low group step counts determine the winners of the match.

Expected Outcomes

- To learn the basic rules of golf
- To play the game with the outcome based on step counts rather than Frisbee throws
- To facilitate social support with group step counts

Equipment and Setting

- Large open space
- One Frisbee and one pedometer per student or group
- One course map per group with a scorecard on the back
- One pencil per group

General Instructions

1. Teach the rules of Frisbee golf. Post the rules and a course map at each tee box. See figure 5.3 for a list of rules that can be used to teach students the basics of Frisbee golf.

2. Use numbered boundary cones for tees. Holes can be boxes, hula hoops, trees, tires, trash cans, or other equipment on the school grounds. Areas around swings and slides can be designated bunkers or out of bounds. Weather permitting, parachutes and mats can also be used as hazards. Draw a course map and provide a copy for every three or four students (see figure 5.4 for an example). Start the groups at different holes to decrease the time spent waiting to tee off. Once a course is established, laminate the maps to increase their longevity. Over time, several courses can be created and alternated.

3. Explain the basics of Frisbee golf to students: Every throw counts as a stroke and the object is to get all the way around the course with as few strokes as possible. Keep the game simple by making hazards count as one stroke.

4. Discuss golf etiquette with students, including "playing through" and waiting for a group to putt out.

5. Give each student a pedometer and a Frisbee. Reset the pedometer as soon as it is fastened in proper position. As students play the course, give feedback and randomly check step counts.

Frisbee golf is played like regular golf. One stroke is counted each time the disc is thrown or when a penalty is incurred. The object of the game is to acquire the lowest score. The following rules dictate play.

- *Tee throws:* Tee throws must be completed within or behind the designated tee area.
- *Lie:* The lie is the spot on or directly under the spot where the previous throw landed.
- *Throwing order:* The player whose disc is the farthest from the hole throws first. The player with the fewest number of throws on the previous hole tees off first.
- *Fairway throws:* Fairway throws must be made with the foot closer to the hole on the lie. A run-up is allowed.
- *Dogleg:* A dogleg is one or more designated trees or poles in the fairway that must be passed on the outside when approaching the hole.
- *Putt throw:* A putt throw is any throw within 10 feet (3 meters) of the hole. A player may not move past the point of the lie in making the putt throw. Falling or jumping putts are not allowed.
- *Unplayable lies:* A disc that comes to rest six feet (1.8 meters) or more above the ground is unplayable. The next throw must be played from a new lie directly under the unplayable lie (one-stroke penalty).
- *Out of bounds:* A throw that lands out of bounds must be played from the point at which the disc went out (one-stroke penalty).
- *Course courtesy:* Do not throw until the players ahead are out of range.
- *Completion of hole:* A disc coming to rest in the hole (box or hoop) or striking the designated hole (tree or pole) constitutes successful completion of that hole.

Figure 5.3   Frisbee golf rules.

6. Determine match winners based on the following:

☐ Highest individual step count

☐ Lowest individual step count (It can be argued that the person who completes the course with the fewest throws will also take the fewest steps.)

☐ Highest group step count

☐ Lowest group step count

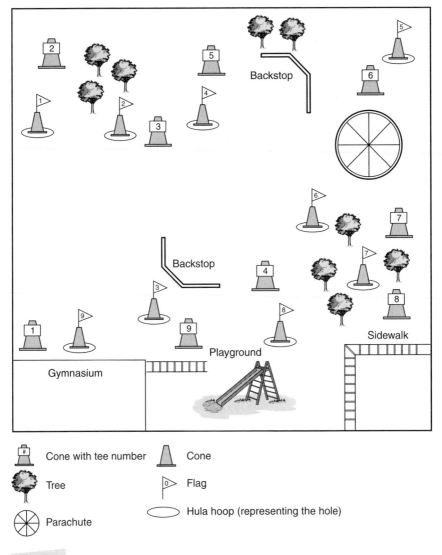

Figure 5.4   Frisbee golf course.

Other Golf Activities

Frisbee golf is not the only way to adapt golf and teach other skills. Soccer golf, throwing golf, and rolling golf are effective ways to allow students to practice skills while increasing activity level. These games are played by the same rules as Frisbee golf, with a few exceptions. An alternative for all of the golf games is to allow students to shoot two rounds under different conditions and compare their step counts for each round. For example, allow third graders to play throwing golf with a tennis ball and then with a Wiffle ball. After the second round, discuss why step counts may be greater during one round than during the other. Another example is to compare a round of Frisbee golf with a round of soccer golf.

Soccer Golf

Soccer golf involves kicking a soccer ball rather than throwing a Frisbee. It is likely that the holes for soccer golf will need to be longer and larger than those used for Frisbee golf, depending on the skill level of the students. An alternative is to use balls that do not travel as well as soccer balls, such as Nerf balls or medium-sized yarn balls, with older students. This alternative allows more holes in a smaller area.

Throwing Golf

Throwing golf is Frisbee golf using a ball rather than a Frisbee. The type of ball used depends on the age of students and the size of the course. Younger students may be able to use balls such as tennis balls that travel well if the course is rather large. A Wiffle ball or small yarn ball is better for older students because it limits the distance of the throws.

Rolling Golf

Rolling golf is played like Frisbee golf, but students roll a ball instead. It can be played with a variety of balls depending on the size of the course and age of the students.

Pedometer Scavenger Hunt

Scavenger hunts while wearing pedometers offer an enjoyable activity that promotes physical activity and integration. You can create numerous hunts to add variety and excitement to lessons while encouraging students to move.

Expected Outcomes

- To provide students with a fun way to accumulate physical activity
- To integrate other academic areas into physical education
- To build students' knowledge of course-related material

Equipment and Setting

- Large open space
- Map of school grounds (see figure 5.1)
- Direction sheet for each landmark
- Clipboard and pencil for each group

General Instructions

1. Set up a course similar to the one described in the orienteering section.

2. Place an envelope at each marker with an index card for each group (laminating these cards will improve their longevity). As was done with orienteering (see figure 5.2*a*), provide a landmark, direction, and distance on each index card, but add a clue to a puzzle that must be solved. This puzzle can be a word, a picture, or a statement, depending on the age of the students. For example, if eight markers are used, each card could contain two of the following letters: PH, YS, IC, AL, AC, TI, VI, and TY. Once all markers have been visited, students will have eight cards that must be unscrambled to spell PHYSICAL ACTIVITY.

Teaching Hints

- To add difficulty, scramble the letters (e.g., PY, IC, AL, TV, II, SH, AY, TC). In this variation, the two letters on the card do not necessarily go side by side in the solution PHYSICAL ACTIVITY.
- Cut pictures into eight pieces and paste the pieces on index cards to create a puzzle.
- Create a puzzle with a physical activity theme to reinforce the concept of lifestyle activity.

Classroom Integration

Consider the following ideas for integrating other subject areas into physical education when developing clues and puzzles.

- Class spelling words for the week
- Characteristics of a country, state, or city the class has studied
- Numbers and math symbols that create a math problem
- Pictures of coins (or fake coins) that must be added to determine a total
- Words that describe a specific animal
- Descriptions of books the class has read
- Pictures of national monuments or landmarks, cut into puzzle pieces

Pedometer Sports Activities

Pedometers can add a different spin to sports activities. Traditionally, sports are designed in a manner that favors the gifted students, making the less-gifted students inactive participants. By incorporating step counts into a sport, accumulating physical activity becomes the focus of the sport rather than athletic ability. Pedometers also allow students to understand how much activity they receive from different sports so teachers can see how active their students are during different units and lessons. The following are examples of sports that can be modified slightly to focus on physical activity and increase the number of steps students accumulate during play.

Alaskan Softball

Arrange students on the field and at bat as shown in figure 5.5. After hitting (off a tee, self-tossed, or pitched) or throwing the ball, the batter runs around his or her team, who are standing in a single-file line. Each time the batter comes to the front of the line, the team gets a point. To increase activity, count the point only if the whole team is running or jumping in place and cheering for the batter.

One player propels the ball by batting or kicking a stationary soccer ball. Teammates are in a line behind the batter. As soon as the ball is batted or kicked, the player begins running around his teammates. The fielding team must run to the student who fields the ball, make a single-file line behind the fielder while running in place, and pass the ball to the end of the line, alternating over the head and between the legs. When the ball gets to the end of the line, the team yells, "Stop!" The batter then stops running and only completed laps count for the batting team's points. Rotate the teams between fielding and batting after five to seven students have batted.

Speed Softball

This game is played by groups of four or five students. Each player tries to see how many runs he or she can score. Players include a catcher, a batter, a pitcher, and one or two fielders as positioned in figure 5.6. The batter chooses how the ball will be put into play (off a tee, self-tossed, a hit pitch, or thrown). Once the ball is in play, the batter begins running back and forth between home plate and a base located where second base would be on a regular softball diamond. The running distance will vary depending on the age and skill level of the students. Each time the batter touches a base, he or she scores a run. (This lets the player score more runs and ensures that they will score at least one run.) While the batter runs between the bases, the fielders, running in place, toss the ball from one to the other and then relay it to the catcher, who is positioned by home plate. When the catcher steps on the plate with the ball in hand, the fielders yell, "Stop!"

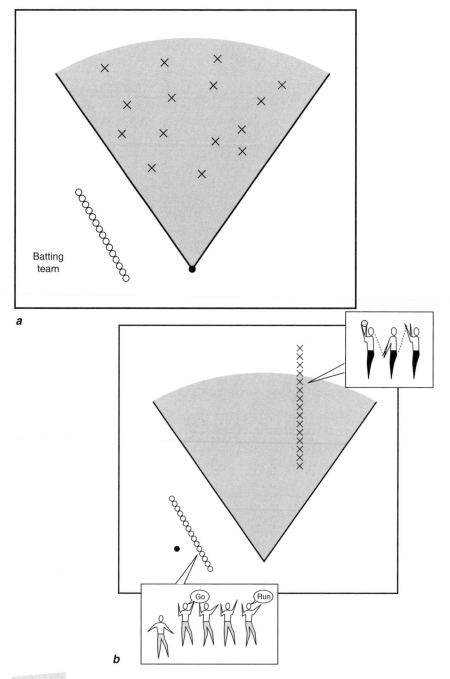

Figure 5.5 Alaskan softball. *(a)* Overhead view of the playing field before the ball is put into play. *(b)* Overhead view of the playing field after the ball is put into play.

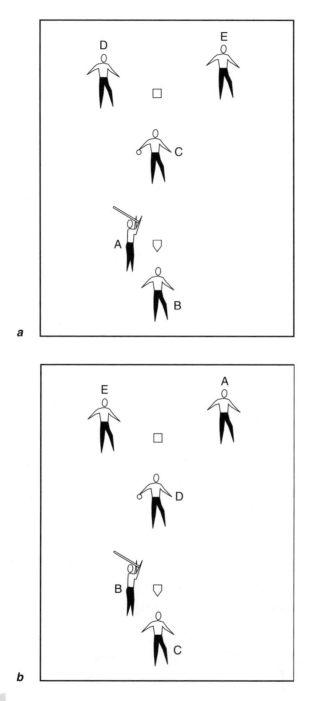

Figure 5.6
Speed softball. *(a)* First rotation and *(b)* second rotation.

The players then rotate so that everyone gets a chance to play every position. To encourage quick rotations, the catcher rotates to batter and puts the ball in play as soon as it is safe to do so. Because the new batter will already be at home plate, this rotation will require all players to hustle to their next position (see the rotation in figure 5.6). Each player's runs, or points, accumulate from one at bat to the next. At the end of the game, each player adds his or her step counts to his or her runs for a total score. This system provides an incentive for students to be active and makes accumulating steps more important than scoring runs.

Sideline Basketball

Sideline basketball is an active lead-up game for students. Facing each other, teams line up on the sidelines of the court. Sideline players must run or jump in place during the game. At the start of the game, four players from each team enter the court and play regulation basketball. Players on the court can pass the ball to sideline players, but sideline players cannot move along the sideline or shoot the ball. Sideline players can pass to each other if they wish, but no more than three passes are permitted before sideline players must pass the ball back to players on the court. After one minute of play, court players quickly join the sideline players at the left end of the line and the next four players enter the court from the right. The remaining sideline players spread out to cover the entire sideline. The ball is out of bounds only if it crosses the end lines, and free throws are granted if a player is fouled while shooting. Scoring is based on points scored and total steps accumulated at the end of the game.

Horse

This traditional game is easily adapted to increase the activity level of all participants. All nonshooters can jog or slide around the area until it is their turn to shoot. In addition, all players can actively rebound the ball and quickly pass it to the next shooter. At the end of the game, the player with the fewest letters receives 250 bonus steps, and the player with the most steps is the winner. This strategy rewards steps (total activity) rather than skill. An alternative is to allow students to play a traditional game of horse (while wearing pedometers), write down their step counts, and then play another game after introducing the new scoring system where accumulating steps is more important than winning the game. The student who shows the biggest increase in step count from the first game to the second game is the overall winner. This scoring system gives all students an opportunity to succeed.

Football Lead-Up Games

Traditionally, football involves brief periods of vigorous activity followed by long periods of inactivity before the next play. Therefore, traditional football is not generally thought of as a lifestyle activity. However, having teams walk or jog in place between plays makes it a much more active game.

An alternative is to play Fanatical Football. This game is a nonstop hybrid of football, team handball, and Ultimate Frisbee. Team A kicks off (or throws) to team B. Team B then attempts to move the ball toward their end zone. When downed (tagged or flagged), the player with the ball instantly (without waiting for the line of scrimmage to set up) becomes the quarterback and looks to pass the ball to a teammate (the pass can be forward or backward). The quarterback cannot be rushed and cannot run more than three steps. Once a pass is completed to a teammate, the receiver can run with the ball until downed, and then he or she becomes the quarterback. This process continues until team B scores a touchdown, team A intercepts, or team B makes an incomplete pass. If team B scores, they immediately turn and kick off. The player who scores is not eligible to kick off, and they do not wait for team A to walk. If team A intercepts, the interceptor immediately becomes the quarterback and his or her team moves toward their end zone. If team B makes an incomplete pass, the member of team A closest to the ball becomes the quarterback and the game continues. To ensure that everyone on the team is involved, keep teams small, use more than one ball, or make a rule that all team members must touch the ball before a team can score.

Scoring can be altered to include step counts in football or football lead-up games. All students wear pedometers, but each team has one pedometer that they rotate among team members. This extra pedometer is the pedometer used to track steps as points. The team rotates the pedometer to allow all students to contribute to the team. A quick rotation takes place at time intervals or after each score. At the end of the game, to emphasize activity and not touchdowns, add team step counts and team scores to determine the team with the most points. These modifications offer simple alternatives to traditional football and allow students to accumulate a substantial number of steps.

Line Soccer

Line soccer is a sport lead-up game that can be modified to increase the number of physical activity opportunities. Divide students into two teams and set up the field as shown in figure 5.7. The setup and play are similar to sideline basketball (see page 92), with a few exceptions.

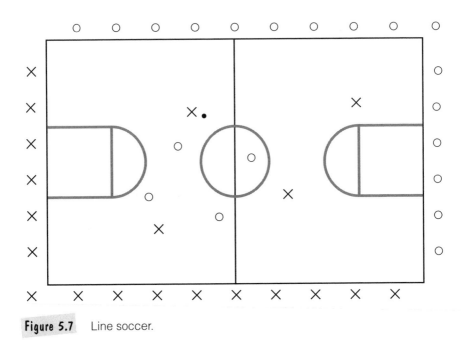

Figure 5.7   Line soccer.

The obvious exceptions are that soccer rules are used rather than basketball rules and players spread out along the end lines as well as the sidelines. Use more than one ball to increase activity levels but no more than three or four for safety reasons. Use Nerf balls instead of regulation soccer balls. Players on the sidelines and end lines are goalies and must prevent the balls from going through their line. Only balls that travel through the line of goalies below chest height are considered goals. To increase activity, all goalies have to walk or jog in place. A variation is to award two bonus goals to the team that has taken the most steps at the end of the game.

Moving Across the Country

When wearing pedometers and recording step counts have become a class routine, one way to show students how much activity they are accumulating during physical education is to implement Moving Across the Country. In this activity, students calculate the total number of miles they walk based on the number of steps they accumulate. Students can track their progress across a smaller designated area (city, county, or state) while the teacher tracks the class's progress across the country. This activity is also an opportunity for teachers to integrate physical education with classroom subjects.

Expected Outcomes

- To teach students the importance of physical activity
- To allow students to record their total steps taken during physical education
- To integrate physical activity into academic subjects, including social studies, math, and English
- To encourage social support through class step counting
- To build students' knowledge of physical activity and class-related material

General Instructions

1. Explain to the class that they will track their progress across the designated area, and you will track the class' progress across the country.
2. Give students a map of a smaller area (city or county) on which to track their progress. A scale in miles or kilometers should be shown on the map. Predrawn routes with the corresponding distances labeled on the map may be useful (e.g., routes from cities to landmarks or from city to city).
3. Allow students to wear pedometers and record their step counts in physical education class.
4. Total the number of steps the class takes during physical education class.
5. Calculate the distance walked using each student's stride length.
6. Allow students to track their progress on their maps using predetermined routes or routes of their choosing.
7. Calculate and chart the total distance for each class on a large map of the country.

Classroom Integration

Moving Across the Country can easily be integrated into classroom lessons. Classroom teachers can calculate steps per mile (or steps per kilometer) and map them during class time. The following are suggestions for integrating this activity into classroom lessons.

- As classes progress to different regions or states, the classroom teacher asks students to find unique geographic characteristics of the state or region. To learn directions, students determine what is north, south, east, or west of their current location.
- An imaginary trip around the country can continue throughout the school year. Establish a route using the classroom teacher's yearly plan for history. As students progress to different areas, the history

of that area becomes a part of a history lesson. Briefly discuss physical activities common in that area or ask questions pertaining to the history lesson at the conclusion of class.

- Teach developmentally appropriate rhythm routines using music from different regions or states. During a rhythm lesson, have students identify the location the class has reached and use music from that region. For example, if the class is in Louisiana, use Cajun music.

- Coordinate art class activities with pedometer use. Have students make posters or other projects that advocate physical activity or healthy lifestyle activities that people in the region they are currently "visiting" might participate in, and use the posters to decorate the gymnasium or school.

- Use computers to assist in all areas of Moving Across the Country. Let students use computers to track their progress, calculate their total number of steps and convert that number to miles or kilometers, research the geography or history of their current location, and make promotional posters advocating active lifestyles.

Pedometer-Enhanced Relays

Adapt relay races to increase activity level. Traditionally, team members who are finished with their leg of the relay stand or sit until the race is over. A way to increase activity in any relay race is to have the waiting team members and finished team members jump and cheer for the runners. The following are examples of relays that require movement by all team members throughout the race. Students can first participate in a traditional relay race while wearing pedometers and then run one of the relays presented in this section. Afterward, students can discuss which method accumulates the most activity.

Kangaroo Relay

Student A, holding a 36-inch (91-centimeter) wand with two hands, runs to the designated area and back. When he or she gets back to the line, student B grabs one end of the wand, with student A holding the other end. Keeping the wand about 12 inches (30 centimeters) off of the ground, they move down the line of teammates, allowing each team member to jump over the wand. At the end of the line, student B, while holding the wand in front with two hands, runs to the designated area and back. Student B and student C hold the wand and move down the line of teammates, again with each team member jumping over the wand (see figure 5.8). Students repeat this process until all team members have carried the wand down and back one time.

Figure 5.8   Kangaroo relay.

Chain Relay

Student A in each team runs to the designated turning point and back. Student A then joins hands with student B, and they both run down and back. Student B then joins hands with student C, and all three run down and back together. This process continues until the entire team joins hands and runs down and back.

Hoop-and-Go Relay

Student A runs to the designated turning point and back carrying a hoop. The entire team then joins hands and passes the hoop to the end of the line by having each player go through the hoop without releasing hands. When the hoop gets to the end of the line, the last student runs down and back and the team must pass through the hoop with hands joined. The race proceeds until all team members have carried the hoop down and back.

Pass-and-Squat Relay

Team members are in a single-file line formation with players standing 7 to 10 feet (2 to 3 meters) apart. Student 1 faces the rest of the team when the relay begins. Student 1 passes a ball to student 2, who quickly passes it back to student 1 and then squats. Student 1 now passes the ball to student 3, who passes it back and squats. Passing and squatting continue until the last student in line receives the ball. This student carries the ball to the front of the line and becomes the passer while all other students move back one place. The race is over when student 1 receives the ball at the back of the line and returns to his or her original position.

Attention Relay

Teams are in single-file line formation at least two arm lengths apart. Team members are 7 to 10 feet (2 to 3 meters) apart. Turning points are designated 10 feet (3 meters) in front of the lane and 10 feet (3 meters) behind the lane. All students are assigned a number, starting at the front of the line. When the teacher calls, "Attention!" all students assume a military-style attention position. The teacher then calls out a number. The student from each team assigned that number steps to the right, runs around the front and back turning points, and returns to his or her original space while the rest of the team runs in place. When the runner returns, all team members and the runner stand at attention. The first team standing at attention wins the point.

Extracurricular Activities

Many schools offer programs for students before school, after school, and during the lunch hour. These extracurricular programs include clubs, intramural sports, and safe places for students to stay before school or while waiting for their parents to pick them up after school, and all provide an opportune time to promote lifestyle activity. The following extracurricular activities or programs use pedometers to promote physical activity.

Physical Activity Clubs

Physical activity clubs (PACs) promote lifestyle activity by making physical activity fun for all students. Like walking clubs and intramural clubs, PACs can be conducted before and after school, as well as during recess. Using pedometers, students track their physical activity during a given period and record their step counts on their own PAC Step Sheet (see page 99).

PAC Step Sheet

Name _____ Teacher _____

Date	Steps	Date	Steps	Date	Steps	Date	Steps

From Robert P. Pangrazi, Aaron Beighle, and Cara L. Sidman, 2007, *Pedometer Power, Second Edition*, (Champaign, IL: Human Kinetics).

Expected Outcomes

- To promote lifestyle activities
- To establish social support through a club that all students are encouraged to join
- To demonstrate to students that all activity is important regardless of the intensity or type

General Instructions

1. Meet with the principal to discuss options for a possible PAC.
2. Brainstorm with other teachers about the PAC.
3. Advertise the program around the school using slogans such as, "Join the PAC," or "Come be a part of the PAC."
4. Design PAC sheets for recording step counts.
5. Speak with local businesspeople about possible donations for PAC shirts or pedometers.
6. Create a schedule for pedometer use. For example, Mrs. Hernandez's class gets the pedometers at recess on Monday and Tuesday, and Mr. O'Connor's class uses them after school on Monday and Wednesday.
7. Discuss the PAC with all classes. Emphasize that all activity is beneficial regardless of intensity.
8. Establish a location for PAC sheets to be stored and pedometers to be returned. Students should record their step count when they return the pedometers and store both in the same location.
9. Appoint students as "pedometer police" for each class. These students are responsible for making sure all pedometers have been returned after the activity period. Give every student an opportunity to serve as a pedometer police officer.
10. Develop ways of promoting the PAC. Possibilities include announcing the names of students who have become PAC members, organizing a charity activitython, and giving small rewards to students who increase their step counts over a given period.

Teaching Hints

- Begin with one grade level to ease implementation.
- At the outset, be visible during activity times. Your presence creates enthusiasm for the program within the school and allows you to maintain quality control.
- Allow students who are not using pedometers for a given day to enter their previous step counts into a spreadsheet and graph their

data during this time. Encourage them to do this quickly and remain active, even on the days they do not use the pedometers.

PAC Charity Walk and Jog

Charity walks and jogs are popular and productive forms of physical activity. By sponsoring a charity walk and jog, the PAC not only promotes lifestyle activity but also involves students with a charity and doing good deeds for others. Encourage parents to participate in these events as a way of promoting lifestyle activity in the community. During the event, let as many students and parents as you can wear pedometers. If possible, get sponsors to base donations on the number of steps participants take.

Expected Outcomes

- To promote physical activity
- To teach charitable behavior
- To encourage social support through a group activity

General Instructions

1. Determine a charity to benefit from the event. Some proceeds could also go toward buying pedometers.
2. Contact the charity representative to discuss your event. This person will be able to provide valuable information regarding promotion, donations, and volunteers to help with the event.
3. Work closely with the charity's personnel to plan the event.
4. At the event, make pedometers available for checkout.
5. At the event, give families a list of family-oriented activities (see chapter 7, page 146).

PAC Family Fun Day

By sponsoring a Family Fun Day, the PAC can designate a day for students and parents to be active and monitor their physical activity. This day showcases physical activity, the PAC, and the physical education program. Students can demonstrate their skills as well as show parents the equipment, including pedometers, used during physical education. This day could become a weekly event. For example, every Saturday morning can be made Family Fun Day at the school. The activities can be rotated based on the physical education lessons taught during the week or the interests of the families in attendance.

Expected Outcomes

- To promote lifestyle activity
- To allow students and parents to use pedometers together, encouraging social support
- To showcase the PAC and the physical education program

General Instructions

1. Determine a date for the event. Set aside an alternative rain date.
2. Send fliers to parents and local businesses. Send these reminders several times before the event.
3. Recruit volunteers.
4. Plan activities and arrange them around booths displaying equipment. Delineate areas for playing. This setup allows families to choose and possibly design activities they enjoy.
5. Organize activities and volunteers.
6. During the event, allow families to check out pedometers.
7. Also, provide handouts containing information on family activities (see chapter 7) and how to buy pedometers.

PAC Moving Across the Country

 Moving Across the Country not only can be a physical education activity but also can be a club activity. The major difference is that PAC Moving Across the Country encourages students to be active on their own time. Allow students to accumulate steps before or after school during extracurricular programs and at recesses. Also, if feasible, students can check out pedometers to take home. Establish a PAC before introducing Moving Across the Country to facilitate this program. Open the PAC to all students because all students are capable of being active. Provide adult supervision for this activity, especially in the initial phases.

Expected Outcomes

- To expose students to the value of physical activity
- To allow students to track their activity and see how much they move
- To provide students with a safe opportunity to accumulate physical activity
- To motivate students to be active
- To integrate physical activity into many academic areas and build knowledge

General Instructions

This activity assumes that a system for checking out pedometers and recording step counts has already been established. First graders may be too young to participate in the program; thus, participants are assumed to be in grades two to six. Before joining a PAC, each student should determine how many of his or her steps equal a mile or kilometer. See chapter 4, pages 64-65, for details on determining stride length.

1. During physical education class, give a brief (no more than five minutes) explanation of the program and how to participate.
2. Hand out a data-recording sheet (see page 99) and teach students how and when to record their steps.
3. Establish a time frame for how often students will trace their progress on the map. Designate one day a week for "finding where you are." For example, every Monday, second graders can calculate their total steps and find their new location. On other days, students in other grades can track their progress across the country during their allotted time.

Classroom Integration

Classroom teachers can use the following ideas to integrate PAC Moving Across the Country into subject areas. These ideas are based on adding the step counts from all students and calculating the total distance traveled by the class. A predetermined route allows teachers to prepare lessons and activities based on where the class is traveling each week. Students can complete the following activities:

- Draw maps of the current location
- Discuss the culture of the closest city
- Determine how far it is to the next city, state, or landmark
- Determine how many steps will be necessary to reach the next area
- Write an essay about the current location
- Study the history of the closest city
- Study the plants, trees, animals, and insects of the current region

Moving Across the Country is an ongoing event in which students can accumulate step counts and miles or kilometers, from the second grade to the sixth grade and beyond if the program is used at the secondary school level. If sufficient pedometers are available, Moving Across the Country can also take place out of school, with students wearing pedometers in the evening and adding those steps to the steps they accumulate in the PAC at school.

Active Intramurals

Lunchtime and after-school intramurals are gaining popularity at elementary schools. The programs provide great opportunities for using pedometers and promoting lifestyle activity. The following is a list of potential methods for emphasizing activity through intramurals.

- Steps-based scoring. Every student wears a pedometer, and pedometer steps are logged on stat sheets after each game. Game points and accumulated step counts (or average step counts) for a team are totaled, and the team with the highest total wins. In this system, a team could be outscored by 50 points and still win by adding its accumulated step counts to its score.

- Steps-based awards. Give awards based on steps and, if desired, traditional awards based on wins and scoring. The following step awards can be given for each intramural season.

  - Most improved stepper. The student whose average step count per game improves the most wins a prize.

  - Most valuable stepper. The student who accumulates the most steps during the intramural season or who averages the most steps per game wins a prize (or a different student can be awarded each prize).

  - The team that averages the most steps per game wins a prize.

  - The team that accumulates the most steps during intramurals wins a prize.

- Awards based on "activityship" (i.e., awards for encouraging others to be active).

These additions to an intramural program emphasize physical activity over skill. This philosophy has two purposes: 1) to promote lifestyle activity and teach students the importance of being active regardless of ability, and 2) to allow students who are less skilled to contribute to the team and experience success.

Schoolwide Pedometer Step Contest

All classrooms in a school can be involved in this contest. The step counts for all students in the class are added and then divided by the number of students. Using the average number of steps eliminates confusion caused by classes of different sizes. This contest is best used within grade levels because of the limited number of pedometers available. For example, all fourth-grade classes compete against each other, and then fifth-grade classes get a turn, and so on. After all classes have collected step counts, you can determine an overall school winner. There are several methods for setting up the contest.

- Students and classroom teachers wear the pedometers for one school day. The following day, another class wears the pedometers.
- Students and classroom teachers wear the pedometers for the entire day, which requires setting a start time. For example, on day 1, students in class A put the pedometers on at 9 a.m. if school starts at 8 a.m. On day 2, class A brings the pedometers back to school, records their step counts, and leaves the pedometers for class B, who puts them on at 9 a.m. Each class follows the same pattern.
- Students and classroom teachers wear the pedometers all day, Monday through Thursday. Tuesday through Friday morning, step counts are recorded, and the pedometers are returned to you on Friday morning. This schedule gives you time to prepare the pedometers for the next Monday-morning class.

Final Thoughts

There is no limit to the number and type of pedometer activities that can be developed by teachers and students. This chapter offers activities that can be adapted to many situations. Ultimately, the goal is to increase awareness about the amount of physical activity that individuals accumulate on a daily basis.

If You Want to Know More . . .

The following list of resouces will provide teachers with supplemental materials related to promoting physical activity for elementary students. These resources include lesson ideas, ideas for teaching health concepts to children, research and information regarding physical activity and elementary-age children, and programs promoting developmentally appropriate sports for children.

Web Sites

www.cdc.gov

The Web site of the Centers for Disease Control and Prevention offers information, statistics, and activities related to physical activity.

www.kidsclick.org

This search engine for children was constructed by librarians. Children can use it to learn about physical activity. In particular, check out the section titled Health & Family.

www.learn-orienteering.org

This site provides ideas for orienteering lessons (e.g., how to use a compass).

www.sports-media.org

Sports Media: Physical Education and Sports for Everyone. This site offers lesson plans, interactive discussions on physical education activities, and related links.

http://reach.ucf.edu/%7Epezone/home.html

PE Zone is a resource for teachers and educators interested in promoting health, physical education, and wellness.

www.education-world.com

This site calls itself the educator's best friend. It provides a searchable database of more than 100,000 education links for teachers, parents, and students.

www.healthfinder.gov/kids

The Web site provided by the Office of Disease Prevention and Health Promotion, U.S. Department of Health and Human Services offers ways for children to be healthy and have fun.

www.ops.org/pe/elem.html

The elementary physical education page of the Omaha Public Schools Web site provides sample activities in which the pedometer can be incorporated.

www.foundation.sdsu.edu/projects/spark/index.html

Sports, Play and Active Recreation for Kids (SPARK) is an elementary physical education program that began as a National Institute of Health research grant. SPARK is a nonprofit organization of San Diego State University, dedicated to improving physical education for children and teachers everywhere.

www.hearteheart.com

This site provides a health and lifestyle curriculum for students in first through third grades. It uses 10 cartoon characters to convey complex physiological functions to teach children about exercise, nutrition, and safety.

www.actionschoolsbc.ca

This Web site details British Columbia's guide to creating a healthy, active school environment.

www.ophea.net

Ontario Physical and Health Education Association offers teacher resources with a free membership.

Article

Hopkins, G. 1998. Let's get physical! *Education World,* www.education-world.com/a_lesson/lesson063.shtml.

Activities for Secondary School and College Students

This chapter describes activities involving pedometers that can easily be integrated into a secondary physical education or college-based curriculum. After a high-quality elementary program, the next logical progression for students is to begin making their own decisions regarding physical activity and consciously thinking about the ramifications of specific behaviors and lifestyles. The activities presented in this chapter are designed to achieve these goals.

Student-Modified Activities Based on Pedometer Steps

Getting students involved in some aspect of creating personalized activities can make the experience meaningful by providing a sense of autonomy. At this level in education, encouraging more critical thinking about how to develop lifetime physical activity habits is an important approach.

Expected Outcomes

- To teach students about physical activity by allowing them to use pedometers to monitor steps
- To encourage students to think about ways to change activities to increase physical activity

Equipment and Setting

One pedometer per student

General Instructions

1. Students wear pedometers during any physical education lesson and record their steps at the end of the lesson.
2. During their next physical education lesson, challenge students to create ways to make the same lesson more active.
3. Provide the following three guidelines for the activities: 1) The activities must be safe, 2) the activities must be at an intensity level that allows all students to participate, and 3) the activities must involve all classmates. For example, students might decide that allowing one bounce while playing volleyball will lengthen rallies and decrease time spent standing around. Or they may decide that a traditional game of softball is not very active and re-create the game. Using pedometers, students can then test the impact of their new rules on their step counts.

Student-Developed Activities

Another strategy for stimulating junior high, high school, and college students to think about physical activity is to have them invent their own games. Many times, this lesson results in new activities that physical education teachers can use with other classes.

© Human Kinetics

Students inventing a new game.

Expected Outcomes

- To allow students to use pedometers to monitor their physical activity level during unique activities
- To have students create their own ways of being active
- To encourage cooperation

Equipment and Setting

- One set of equipment per group scattered around the teaching area (For example, one set may consist of a Nerf ball, a cone, a softball glove, and a jump rope. Another set may be a scooter, a playground ball, and a compass.)
- One pedometer per student

General Instructions

1. Separate students wearing pedometers into groups of four to six.
2. Each group picks up their equipment.
3. Direct the groups to invent a game that uses the equipment and follows these rules:
   - ☐ Everyone must be active and participate in the activity.
   - ☐ The activity must be safe, and the equipment must be used in an acceptable manner but not necessarily for its intended use.
   - ☐ To add challenges, include the rule, "At least one piece of equipment has to be used in a manner different from its traditional use." For example, use a racket to catch a ball rather than to strike a ball. Also, groups can be asked to minimize the number of rules they use.
4. Give the groups 15 to 20 minutes to create the game and practice it while monitoring their steps. They may find it necessary to make changes based on the steps accumulated during the activity.
5. After the groups have created a game, let them share the activity with each other.
6. Discuss why some activities are more active than others.
7. Discuss why a group or person may be more active during one activity than another group or person.

Student-Designed Pedometer Orienteering Course

Chapter 5 described a pedometer orienteering course designed by the teacher. Because the goal in secondary physical education is to teach students to participate in instructional settings, this lesson places the responsibility on students to design an orienteering course.

Expected Outcomes

- To teach students to use a pedometer as a tool for both assessing physical activity and aiding in orienteering, a lifestyle activity
- To provide students with experience in designing and navigating their own orienteering course
- To expose students to the importance of cooperation

Equipment and Setting

- Create a blank map of the school grounds or area used for orienteering, with boundaries clearly marked. The orienteering area should be safe from hazards.
- Each student should have a pedometer.
- Design a course and introduce orienteering. Depending on school policy, this can be done on or off of school property.

General Instructions

1. During the initial lesson, let students know that they will design a course that will be used by other groups. They need to carefully monitor their steps so they can list the steps required during orienteering. Include a discussion about how to develop instructions and marker placement.

2. During the ensuing lessons, divide the class into groups of three or four and give them time to map their course and create instructions and markers.

3. Students draw their courses on a blank map of the area. This step may take two or three class periods depending on the area. However, because students walk to create their courses, they will be active.

4. Remind students to estimate the number of steps required and then test their estimates to determine the actual number to list on the map.

5. Once all groups have finished designing their courses and have documented the approximate number of steps it takes to complete the course, review the maps to ensure clarity of instructions. This prevents ridicule from peers and embarrassment during the following step.

6. The next step is to exchange maps and have students attempt to navigate the courses created by other groups. Groups use the instructions provided by the mapmakers to navigate the course.

7. Groups also look to see if the number of steps taken by the other group matches their count. Discuss factors that can influence steps (e.g., stride length, cutting corners).

8. To add a challenge, ask groups to design a course that will take approximately 2,500 steps or create a course that will be approximately one mile, or 1.6 kilometers. For consistency, groups can designate one member as the "stepper" for measuring distance. See pages 64-65 for details on measuring stride length.

Activity Exploration

 This activity is designed to help students explore different types of physical activity. Activities can be demanding or relaxing, require aerobic fitness or motor coordination. This activity encourages students to discover such differences.

Expected Outcomes

- To encourage students to participate in new activities
- To teach students how to monitor the number of steps accumulated during a variety of activities
- To allow students to express their findings and thoughts through writing

Equipment and Setting

One pedometer per student

General Instructions

1. Discuss lifestyle activity and its importance (refer to page 4). Allow the class to brainstorm and think of activities that can be classified as lifestyle activities.
2. Explain that the assignment is to wear a pedometer while participating in two lifestyle activities, one of which is new to them.
3. After participating in each activity for the same amount of time (20 to 30 minutes), students record step counts for each activity.
4. Students complete a one-page paper and include the following points:
   - An explanation of the activities and why they are considered lifestyle activities
   - The amount of activity accumulated while participating in the activities
   - Whether they think one of the activities was better for them and why
   - Why they did or did not enjoy each activity

Peer Teaching

Peer teaching helps students better understand activities that can be used throughout the lifespan. Students should learn how some types of activity offer more health benefits than others.

Expected Outcomes

- To encourage students to think of a variety of lifestyle activities
- To give students an opportunity to teach lifestyle activities
- To provide students with numerous options for lifestyle activities
- To provide students an understanding of how much activity various lifestyle activities provide

Equipment and Setting

One pedometer per student

General Instructions

1. Discuss lifestyle activities with the class, including examples of lifestyle activity.
2. Assign students to present, or teach, a lifestyle activity to the class or a small group.
3. Activities that can be participated in during physical education are desired. However, if the physical education program does not have the equipment or facilities, the activity can be presented and discussed without participation.
4. After teaching the activity, the group or class participates in the activity for 10 minutes while wearing pedometers.
5. The steps taken for each activity are documented on a card.
6. A discussion about the effectiveness of the activity and ways to modify it to increase the amount of physical activity follows. Students can test the effectiveness of their suggestions for increasing physical activity.
7. After students have presented their activities, they can list all of them and the number of steps accumulated in 10 minutes of each. They can take this sheet home or place it in a student portfolio.

Physical Education Activities

The following series of activities should first be done during physical education classes. Once students become familiar with the activities, give them the option of checking out the pedometers and using these activities to measure daily physical activity during school and outside of school.

Establishing Baseline Step Counts for Daily Physical Activity

Obtaining an average daily baseline step count provides a meaningful reference point to build from by setting step goals or to maintain if it is sufficient for health. Without information about where an individual is starting from with regard to his or her activity level, it is more difficult to make an effective plan to improve.

Expected Outcomes

- To allow students to monitor their own daily physical activity level using a pedometer and establish their average daily steps
- To encourage students to be active

Equipment and Setting

One pedometer per student

General Instructions

1. Provide each student with a Baseline and Goal-Setting Log (see page 117). Students will also use this sheet for Pedometer Goal Setting and Individual Intervention Programs.
2. Encourage students to track their step counts for four days and calculate their average daily physical activity.

Pedometer Goal Setting

Pedometers are valuable for practicing the self-management skill of goal setting because of their ability to provide immediate and objective feedback on physical activity levels. However, as discussed in chapter 4, arbitrary, unrealistic step goals are not recommended. This activity focuses on teaching effective goal-setting strategies to achieve optimal results.

Expected Outcomes

- To teach the process of goal setting
- To encourage students to be physically active
- To teach students how to use pedometers to monitor their progress toward set goals
- To allow students to be successful and reach realistic goals

Equipment and Setting

One pedometer per student

 **Baseline and Goal-Setting Log**

Baseline Physical Activity Level

Trials	Day 1	Day 2	Day 3	Day 4	Total steps/ 4 days
1					
2					
				Average daily steps	

Goal Setting

Average daily steps	Goal (percentage increase)	Goal (step counts)

Individual Intervention Program

Trials	Day 1	Day 2	Day 3	Day 4	Total steps/ 4 days
1					
2					
				New average daily steps	

To calculate the percentage change use the following equation:
[new average daily steps − average (daily steps) + average daily steps] × 100 = percentage change

From Robert P. Pangrazi, Aaron Beighle, and Cara L. Sidman, 2007, *Pedometer Power, Second Edition*, (Champaign, IL: Human Kinetics).

General Instructions

1. During physical education or a college health and fitness course, briefly discuss goal setting with step counts. See chapter 4 for a discussion of goal setting.

2. Using the average number of steps generated while self-monitoring baseline activity, students should set an achievable goal for themselves.

3. Each time they use a pedometer, they should check their progress toward their goal and make adjustments accordingly.

Goal-Setting Menu

Another way to teach goal setting is to provide a menu of choices from which students may choose. This option explores goal setting in more depth.

Expected Outcomes

- To provide students with an opportunity to experience a variety of relevant goal-setting techniques based on goal theory (specificity, attainability, difficulty, and proximity)

- To determine a preferred type of goal-setting method for future pedometer use

Equipment and Setting

- One pedometer per student

- Opportunity to take the pedometer home for an extended time

General Instructions

1. Students record their daily step count for a minimum of four days to obtain a baseline.

2. Students select the goal type from the goal-setting menu (see figure 6.1) that they think is most likely to result in increased activity levels. Students should track their step counts for one week, trying to achieve their goal.

3. Taking the average step count from the previous week, students repeat step 2 using a different goal-setting method for one week, for a minimum of four weeks.

4. After trying at least four methods, students compare and contrast the types of step goals and determine what they liked and disliked about the different ways to set goals. More specifically, they will compare their average daily and total weekly step counts from

Goal-Setting Menu

Week	Goal type	Description	Example
1	Step goal	3,000-4,000 steps above baseline (~30 min. of activity)	Baseline: 4,000 steps Goal: 7,000 steps
2	Percentage goal	Up by 10% increments	Baseline: 4,000 steps 2-week goal: 4,400 steps 4-week goal: 4,840 steps
3	Steps/min. goal	Men: 96 steps/min. Women: 107 steps/min. (Tudor-Locke, Sisson, Collova, Lee, & Swan, 2005)	Baseline: 86 steps/min. for 30 min. = 2,580 steps Goal: 100 steps/min. for 30 min. = 3,000 steps
4	Step increment goal	Up by a specific number of steps (e.g., add 1,000 steps every two weeks)	Baseline: 4,000 steps 2-week goal: 5,000 steps 4-week goal: 6,000 steps 6-week goal: 8,000 steps
5	* Time goal	Up by a specific number of min. (e.g., 10 min.)	Baseline: 20 min. Goal: 30 min.
6	* Mileage goal	Up by mileage (e.g., 0.5 mile/week [0.8 km/week])	Baseline: 2 miles (3.2 km) 1-week goal: 2.5 miles (4 km) 2-week goal: 3 miles (4.8 km)
7	Group goals	Combine the step counts of the entire class and set a step goal as a group	Class baseline: 150,000 steps (25 students) Group end-of-semester goal: 200,000 (up by ~2,000 steps per student)
8	Other		Students create their own goal-setting technique

* Must have pedometers with these features included.

Figure 6.1 Sample goal-setting menu.

each of the four weeks and determine which type of goal-setting technique resulted in the highest step counts. They should write a reflection essay regarding why they think the specific goal type resulted in the greatest amount of physical activity.

Individual Intervention Programs

Based on their baseline data and corresponding goals, students can develop an individual intervention program (IIP). This is their plan of action for increasing their accumulated physical activity. Examples for outside-of-school interventions are walking to school or simply spending more time outside during the evening. This activity assumes students have already established their baseline step counts and have set achievable, yet challenging, goals.

Expected Outcomes

- To expose students to interventions
- To teach students to plan for physical activity
- To allow students to use pedometers to assess the effectiveness of their IIP

Equipment and Setting

One pedometer per student

General Instructions

1. During physical education or a college personal health and fitness course, discuss physical activity intervention programs. Be sure to emphasize that these are simply plans for increasing physical activity. Also, provide examples of ways to intervene, both during physical education, during school, and outside of school (see figure 6.2). For example, rather than sitting for the entire lunch period, students can walk and talk with friends to increase physical activity.
2. Instruct each student to develop his or her own intervention program.
3. Using pedometers and their baseline step counts, students can test the effectiveness of their program.
4. Ask students to write a short paper explaining why they think their program was or was not effective.
5. Encourage students to continue steps 2 and 3 to find a method that works for them.

- Do chores three days per week rather than one day per week.
- Walk the dog every day.
- Play physically active games or walk rather than sit when you are given free time at school (lunchtime or break time).
- Go for a hike with your parents.
- Rake yards or shovel driveways in your neighborhood.
- Start a family basketball game.
- Walk to school rather than have a parent drive you (with parents' permission).
- Invent dances or dance routines and practice them.
- Organize a physical activity group in your neighborhood, and play a different game or activity each day.
- Use stairs instead of elevators.
- Snowboard or sled.

Figure 6.2   Intervention strategies.

Hypothesis Testing With Pedometers

 Using pedometers to integrate the scientific process into physical education is easy and provides a way to reinforce concepts learned in the classroom while continuing to work toward the goal of physical education—promoting lifestyle activity. This activity is described for individual students, but students can also work with partners or in small groups if desired.

Expected Outcomes

- To reinforce the scientific process through physical education
- To teach students to critically think about physical activity

Equipment and Setting

Enough pedometers for students to test their hypotheses (one pedometer per student or enough pedometers for students to check out)

General Instructions

1. Briefly review the scientific process, or hypothesis testing.
2. Give students examples of using pedometers for hypothesis testing. For example, pedometers can be used to prove or disprove these statements:

☐ Athletes take more steps during football practice than during volleyball practice.

☐ Students take more steps during an orienteering lesson than a football lesson.

☐ Students are more active than parents.

3. Students create a hypothesis and turn it in with a corresponding method for proving or disproving it using a pedometer or another creative technique. Review the assignments for feasibility and appropriateness.

4. Once you have approved the projects, students can check out one or two pedometers to use to carry out their test. If pedometers are limited, this can be an ongoing project.

5. After carrying out their test, students write a paper discussing the project and their results.

Learning About the Activity Guidelines

Because activity guidelines state that youth should be active for at least 60 minutes each day, many students want to know how many steps they take in 30 to 60 minutes. This question provides an effective segue into lessons using pedometers during physical education and also outside of physical education. Remind students that these guidelines are **minimum** daily recommendations.

Expected Outcomes

- To teach students the physical activity guidelines
- To see how many steps can be accumulated in 30 to 60 minutes

Equipment and Setting

One pedometer per student

General Instructions

1. Create a handout that briefly explains the physical activity guidelines for adolescents (see chapter 1).

2. Discuss the guidelines and how students can use them.

3. Using pedometers, students record their step counts during a lesson lasting approximately 30 minutes and record the data.

4. Discuss if this is a good way to determine the number of steps taken in 30 minutes. If students do not think that the type of activity affects step counts, introduce and discuss how the type and intensity of activity will influence the number of steps taken.

5. Continue steps 3 and 4 for several lessons. After several varied lessons (basketball, orienteering, tennis), students will begin to understand that the number of steps taken can vary depending on the activity and that even leisurely walking, such as walking during an orienteering lesson, accumulates a substantial number of steps in 30 minutes.

Pedometer Activities for College Students

Although all of the activities in this chapter can be used with college students, the following are designed specifically for this target group. College students are in a somewhat unique situation in that they are typically away from home for the first time, which means they must make independent decisions regarding their health behaviors. They are also unique in that their environment and subsequently, their behaviors, are distinctly different from what they would be in more "real life" situations. For example, many college students live with a roommate in a dormitory, are forced to park far away from the buildings, eat in a cafeteria-style all-you-can-eat setting, are surrounded by many unhealthy behaviors, and are heavily influenced by peers. This scenario is not ideal for promoting healthy behaviors, and many college students have the idea that they are indestructible, so they do not consider how their behavior now will affect them in the future. It is important to teach students the relationship between personal behaviors and lifelong health and wellness and help them develop self-management skills so they can make healthy decisions throughout life. Increasing awareness and knowledge, promoting self-efficacy, encouraging social support, and finding ways to increase enjoyment and motivation for healthy living should be at the forefront of pedometer activity planning. Creative ideas for using pedometers in a one- to three-credit college-based general education fitness and wellness course follow.

The intent of this section is to give you a variety of ideas from which to choose in order to enhance student enjoyment of physical activity and the use of pedometers. Each of the activities in this section includes a corresponding figure that details the instructions, activities to be performed, and questions for your students to complete either in or out of class.

Pedometers 101

A basic introduction to pedometers is always a good way to start the semester or class. It gives students an opportunity to understand the features of the device, as well as its limitations, so that they are better equipped to interpret step-count readings in future use.

Expected Outcomes

- To introduce students to pedometers
- To increase awareness of the proper use, features, and limitations of pedometers
- To encourage students to think critically and to become independent problem solvers

Equipment and Setting

- One pedometer per student
- Pen or pencil
- Track

General Instructions

1. Have students complete the Pedometers 101 activities on pages 125-126 and respond to all of the questions for full credit on the assignment.
2. Be sure their pedometers are secured in a vertical position on the waistband or belt, directly above the midline of their right thigh. Have them fasten the safety strap by clipping it to their clothing. See page 41 in chapter 3 for pedometer placement options.

Active vs. Inactive Day

Getting students to think about how their daily choices have a significant effect on their activity levels can be achieved through a hands-on activity. Comparing the extremes of being as active as possible versus as inactive as possible in daily lifestyle activity choices can be an eye-opener for many students.

Expected Outcome

To demonstrate the impact of lifestyle activities on overall daily step counts

Equipment and Setting

- One pedometer per student
- Opportunity to take the pedometer home for at least two days

General Instructions

1. Have students complete the Active vs. Inactive Day pedometer assignment on page 127.
2. Allot class time to discuss students' reactions to this activity.

Pedometers 101

1. Pedometer calibration

   How does the pedometer register steps?

   a. Set your pedometer to zero, and be sure it is securely closed.

   b. Walk 50 steps as normally as possible in a **straight** line. **Do not** change your gait just because you are counting or trying to get the pedometer to register!

   c. After the 50 steps, carefully open the pedometer and record the number of steps on the line below.

      Number of steps recorded: _____

   d. Why might the pedometer register more or fewer than 50 steps?

      Reason: _____

2. Four-lap walk guess

   Guess how many steps and how many minutes you think it will take to walk four laps (1 mile, or 1,600 meters) at a moderately intense pace. Record below.

   a. Step count guess: _____

   b. Time guess: _____

      Reset your pedometer to zero and walk the distance at a moderately brisk pace. Record your final step count and time.

   c. Actual step count: _____

   d. Actual time: _____

      Record the difference between your guess and your actual step count and time (indicate if you overestimated or underestimated).

   e. Step count difference: _____

   f. Time difference: _____

   g. Write a brief reaction to this activity (e.g., Were you surprised at how close or how far off you were in your guesses? What factors might have played a role in your actual step count or time? What did you learn from this activity?)

      _____

      _____

      _____

(continued)

From Robert P. Pangrazi, Aaron Beighle, and Cara L. Sidman, 2007, *Pedometer Power, Second Edition*, (Champaign, IL: Human Kinetics).

Pedometers 101 *(continued)*

3. High intensity vs. low intensity

   Answer the following question **before** you perform the activity.

   a. Do you think walking one lap will produce the same step count as running one lap (or walking at a more intense pace)? Why or why not?

   _____

   _____

   _____

   b. Reset your pedometer to zero. Walk or run one lap as fast as you can and record your step count.

      High-intensity step count: _____

   c. Reset your pedometer to zero and walk or run one lap at a slower, less-intense pace. Record your step count.

      Low-intensity step count: _____

   d. Write a brief reaction to this activity (e.g., Were you surprised at how different or similar the step counts were for the same distance covered? What are possible reasons for doing this activity? What did you learn?)

   _____

   _____

   _____

4. New activity

   Develop a new pedometer activity that could be done inside or outside of class that would be interesting as well as provide a learning experience. Explain why, and be creative!

From Robert P. Pangrazi, Aaron Beighle, and Cara L. Sidman, 2007, *Pedometer Power, Second Edition,* (Champaign, IL: Human Kinetics).

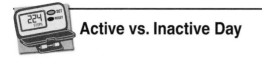

Active vs. Inactive Day

Inactive Day Instructions

1. Wear a pedometer for one full day, while consciously trying to be as inactive as possible during your normal everyday activities. For example, take the elevator instead of the stairs, park as close to a building as you can, take the bus to school, and get rides as often as you can.
2. Complete the Inactive Step Log.

Inactive Step Log

Date	Total number of steps	Lifestyle activities you avoided	Comments

Provide additional comments about your inactive day: _____
_____
_____

Active Day Instructions

1. Wear the pedometer for one full day, while consciously trying to be as **active** as possible during your normal everyday activities. For example, take the stairs instead of the elevator, park far away from a building, and walk to school instead of taking the bus.
2. Complete the Active Step Log.

Active Step Log

Date	Total number of steps	Lifestyle activities	Comments

Provide additional comments about your active day: _____
_____
_____

Final Reaction

After completing both days, write about your reaction to this activity. Be thorough and specific in your response to earn full credit. Write in complete sentences using proper grammar and correct spelling.

From Robert P. Pangrazi, Aaron Beighle, and Cara L. Sidman, 2007, *Pedometer Power, Second Edition*, (Champaign, IL: Human Kinetics).

Guess and Walk

Until students use pedometers on a regular basis, it is difficult to predict the number of steps accumulated when walking various distances. This skill can be helpful in the future when making physical activity choices, and it can also make it more fun.

Expected Outcomes

- To encourage students to be active
- To give students an opportunity to practice estimating step counts

Equipment and Setting

- One pedometer per student
- Map of walking route for each student
- Pen or pencil

General Instructions

Have students complete the Guess and Walk pedometer assignment on page 129.

Awareness Activities

The pedometer activities in this section increase student awareness of personal behavior and the development of self-management skills. They examine the physical aspect of behavior change as well as other dimensions such as social, intellectual, spiritual, emotional, and environmental. Secondary and college-aged students will likely face issues of independence and making decisions about personal health behaviors. Increasing knowledge and awareness, developing self-management skills, and creating a supportive environment conducive to health and wellness at an early age are important in developing a lifetime of positive behaviors.

Interview

The environment in which we live plays a big role in our behaviors, with social support being one important element. The basis for the interview activity is to get students thinking about the role other individuals play in their health behaviors.

Guess and Walk

Procedures

1. Before starting, guess the number of steps you think it will take for you to walk to each destination. Write these guesses in the step-count guess column in the step log.
2. Record your starting step count in the space provided before you begin walking.
3. Walk to each destination with at least one other person from class (see map provided for walking route).
4. Monitor how the pace makes you feel to determine how intensely you are walking.
5. When you arrive at each destination, record the step count (do not reset the pedometer).
6. Follow steps 3 through 5 until you return to the starting point.
7. Calculate the number of steps taken to reach each destination by determining the difference between step-count totals.
8. Subtract your step-count guess from the actual number of steps taken and record the number in the How far off were you? column. Indicate if you overestimated or underestimated with a + or –, respectively. See the step log examples below.
9. When you are finished, record comments about this activity at the bottom of the log.
10. Submit your completed log to your instructor.

Guess and Walk Sample Step Log

Destination	Step-count guess	Starting step count	Ending step count	Actual step count	How far off were you?	Intensity
Example: 1. Bed → Class	400	800	1,600	800	–400	Low
Example: 2. Class → Front door of building	900	1,300	1,800	500	+400	Mod.
1. Godwin Hall → Convocation Center						
2. Convocation Center → College Center Lobby						
3. College Center Lobby → Weaver Hall						
4. Weaver Hall → Market One						
5. Market One → Stadium Entrance						
6. Stadium → Godwin Hall						
Comments						

Modify the log to fit your walking route. Attach it to your map that includes arrows indicating the route, the start, and the finish.

From Robert P. Pangrazi, Aaron Beighle, and Cara L. Sidman, 2007, *Pedometer Power, Second Edition*, (Champaign, IL: Human Kinetics).

Expected Outcome

To increase awareness of the impact of others on personal health behaviors

Equipment and Setting

- One pedometer per student
- Opportunity to take the pedometer home for up to two days

General Instructions

1. Discuss the following with students before starting the activity. An important part of developing health behaviors that last a lifetime is to surround oneself with a supportive environment. Parents, guardians, siblings, and peers have a significant influence on behavior, especially on young people.

2. Have students select a person in their life who influences their behavior (e.g., parent, friend, sibling).

3. The student gives that person a pedometer and explains to them the following procedures:

   a. Wear the pedometer for one full day without changing your normal daily activities.

   b. Record your step count for the day.

   c. Set a step goal for the following day and explain why you chose that goal.

   d. Wear the pedometer the following day and try to achieve your goal.

   e. Record your step count for the second day.

   f. Indicate the difference between your goal step count and your actual step count.

   g. Explain why you think you met or did not meet your step goal.

   h. Explain what, if anything, you would do differently next time when setting a step goal.

   i. Complete the interview table (see page 131).

4. Students use the information gathered to answer these final questions:

   a. Do you believe that the activity levels of your influential person affect your activity levels? Why or why not?

   b. After reviewing how your influential person set his or her step goal, would you set yours in a similar manner? Why or why not?

   c. Think about your environment and how influential this person is. What impact has he or she had on your physical activity level? Explain.

 **Interview Table**

	Step count	Goal
Normal day		
Goal day		
Difference in step count		
Explanation		

The Popular 10,000-Step Goal

The media has promoted a daily 10,000-step goal to motivate people to be active. However, this step goal is not necessary for every individual to achieve, especially if baseline step counts are low and the goal is to improve health rather than achieve optimal fitness. If the purpose of using pedometer goal-setting practices is to promote adherence to physical activity, individuals must be armed with the knowledge of what daily step count will best suit their current activity levels and future goals.

Expected Outcome

Because of the popularity of the 10,000-step daily goal, the purpose of this activity is to increase awareness of and experience the amount of activity necessary to achieve 10,000 steps.

Equipment and Setting

- One pedometer per student
- Opportunity to take the pedometer home
- The activity must be presented differently for students who typically attain 10,000 steps per day and those who do not.

General Instructions

1. For one full day, students wear a pedometer while keeping all of their activities the same. Students record all daily activities that take more than 10 minutes on the 10,000-Step Log (see page 133) and then record this total "normal day" step count.
2. Students who achieved fewer than 10,000 steps should strive to attain 10,000 steps the next day. They should record the activities they added in order to achieve this step count. Designate all additional activity with an asterisk.
3. Students who achieved 10,000 steps or more, discuss or write about why they think they easily achieved this step count.
4. Have both groups of students discuss or write about whether they think 10,000 steps is appropriate for everyone, as well as their reaction to this activity.
5. After student reactions are completed, explain that 10,000 steps (which is approximately equal to five miles [8 kilometers]) originated as a business slogan in Japan and that people can still meet the health recommendations for physical activity without attaining 10,000 steps (depending on their lifestyle daily activity patterns: sedentary vs. active job, walking vs. driving to classes, and so on). Also, explain that a goal of 10,000 steps may be too high for some people (e.g., sedentary adults), yet too low for others (e.g., children).

10,000-Step Log

Reminders

- Be sure the pedometer is secured in a vertical position with the lid closed. The pedometer will not accurately measure your steps if you are wearing something with a loose waistband. Loose waistbands can cause the pedometer to shift into a horizontal position and miss steps.
- Be sure to press the reset button in the morning.
- Secure the safety strap to your clothes to prevent loss and limit damage.
- Please, on the normal day, do not increase your physical activity just because you are wearing the pedometer. Keep your activity level as normal as possible.
- Be sure to record activity that lasts longer than 10 minutes in the appropriate column.

Day	Date	Total number of steps	Activity (>10 min.)	Check here if you did anything out of the ordinary	Comments (If you did extra activity, describe the type and amount here.)
Example: Normal day	5/22	6,225	20 min. jog	√	• Went for a 30-min. horseback ride. • Took a 30-min. dance lesson.
Normal day					
10,000- step day					

Additional comments:

From Robert P. Pangrazi, Aaron Beighle, and Cara L. Sidman, 2007, *Pedometer Power, Second Edition,* (Champaign, IL: Human Kinetics).

Rain or Shine?

Without a doubt, the environment affects health behaviors. Weather conditions influence an individual's decision whether or not to be physically active. This activity demonstrates the extent of this influence.

Expected Outcomes

To increase awareness of the effect of climate on step counts

Equipment and Setting

- One pedometer per student
- Opportunity to take the pedometer home
- A day of sunshine and a day of rain or inclement weather where going outside is typically kept to a minimum

General Instructions

1. For one full sunny day, students wear a pedometer and record their step counts and daily activities that last longer than 10 minutes (the 10,000-Step Log on page 133 can be adapted to normal day vs. rainy day).
2. For one full rainy day or inclement day (e.g., snowy, extremely cold, windy), students wear a pedometer and record their step counts and activities that last longer than 10 minutes.
3. When completed, students compare and contrast the step counts and physical activities for each day and discuss or write about their reaction and what they learned from performing this activity.

30 Minutes

The Surgeon General's guidelines for physical activity and health include a 30-minute recommendation (either continuous or in 10-minute bouts) of moderate intensity activity on most days of the week. Performing a variety of activities for 30 minutes while wearing a pedometer can increase awareness of the step counts associated with different types of activities.

Expected Outcomes

- To determine how many steps students take while participating in 30 minutes of a variety of activities
- To increase awareness of how the U.S. Surgeon General's guideline of 30 minutes of moderately intense activity can be met but yield different step counts depending on the type of activity performed

Equipment and Setting

One pedometer per student

General Instructions

1. Have students select four different activities that can be measured with a pedometer to perform continuously for 30 minutes (e.g., walking, jogging, step aerobics, hiking, racquetball).

2. Record the step counts for each 30-minute activity period and discuss reasons why the counts varied for the same amount of activity time.

Pedometer Thoughts

At the secondary and college levels, encouraging more critical thought regarding the use of pedometers to measure physical activity and motivate people to be active for a lifetime is important. This activity delves into the pedometer literature and allows for discussion to enhance learning and make the information more applicable to students' daily lives.

Expected Outcomes

- To learn basic information regarding the history and use of pedometers

- To read current literature on pedometers

- To encourage critical thinking

Equipment and Setting

To complete this assignment, students need copies of two research articles: "Taking Steps Toward Increased Physical Activity: Using Pedometers to Measure and Motivate" (Tudor-Locke, 2002) and "How Many Steps/Day Are Enough? Preliminary Pedometer Indices for Public Health" (Tudor-Locke & Bassett, 2004). See the references at the end of this chapter for complete information on the journals in which these articles appear.

General Instructions

1. Ask students to read both articles by a specific date.

2. Assign the content questions presented on page 136 for both articles. These can be completed in class or outside of class.

3. Facilitate small-group discussions and then hold a class discussion specifically on the discussion questions presented on page 136.

Pedometer Thoughts

Students should be able to answer the following questions after reading the pedometer article "Taking Steps Toward Increased Physical Activity: Using Pedometers to Measure and Motivate" by Tudor-Locke, 2002.

Content Questions

1. Who was the first to conceptualize pedometers? Where did he purchase his first pedometer?
2. Which country has been using pedometers to assess and increase physical activity for more than 30 years?
3. How did 10,000 steps first come about?
4. Should everyone strive to achieve 10,000 steps per day?
5. Pedometers have been around for a long time. Why are they widely accepted and used now? Give three reasons.
6. How do pedometers work? What do they measure?
7. What are the limitations of pedometers?
8. According to research, when do pedometers consistently show more error?
9. How can you "quickly validate" a pedometer?
10. If someone is interested in determining patterns of daily physical activity, how long should he or she wear the pedometer and record steps?

Discussion Questions

1. Do you think people alter their behavior just because they are wearing a pedometer? Why or why not? What does research show on this, and what is this called?
2. What population or populations do you think are most likely to benefit from and enjoy using pedometers? Why?

Pedometer Step Classifications

Classifications are important because researchers and practitioners need specific quantitative indices (cut points) for screening, surveillance, intervention, and program evaluation. They can also be used to monitor, compare, and track population trends of sedentarism.

From Robert P. Pangrazi, Aaron Beighle, and Cara L. Sidman, 2007, *Pedometer Power, Second Edition*, (Champaign, IL: Human Kinetics).

Classifications	Number of steps/ day
Sedentary lifestyle index	<5,000
Low active (typical daily activity excluding sports and exercise)	5,000-7,999
Somewhat active (includes some volitional activities or elevated occupational demands)	7,500-7,999
Active	≥10,000
Highly active	≥12,500

Tudor-Locke and Bassett, 2004.

Important Points to Remember

- The goal of 10,000 steps is not for everyone.
  - ☐ It is too high for older adults and people with chronic diseases, who average 3,500 to 5,500 steps per day.
  - ☐ It is too low for children (recommendations are 11,000 steps per day for girls and 13,000 steps per day for boys).
  - ☐ If 6,000 to 7,000 steps is indicative of usual daily activity, then the addition of 3,000 to 4,000 steps per day of moderate intensity results in 9,000 to 11,000 steps per day (in agreement with the 10,000 steps per day goal).
  - ☐ However, some people can accumulate 30 minutes of moderately intense activity with fewer than 10,000 steps per day.
- Self-directed goal setting is recommended.
- Improvement in health can be found with 2,500 to 4,300 steps over baseline.
- Thirty minutes of walking equals 3,000 to 4,000 steps.

Discussion Questions

1. For nonresearch purposes, do you think it is important to classify individuals according to their daily step count? Why or why not?
2. Would you recommend the goal of 10,000 steps per day to anyone? If so, who and why?

From Robert P. Pangrazi, Aaron Beighle, and Cara L. Sidman, 2007, *Pedometer Power, Second Edition,* (Champaign, IL: Human Kinetics).

Physical Activity and Culture

As in Pedometer Thoughts, this activity challenges students to think at a higher level by reading and discussing research on pedometers, specifically related to culture. The required reading demonstrates the role the cultural environment plays in physical activity behaviors. This can broaden students' perspectives on the contributing factors to sedentary living.

Expected Outcomes

- To explore the effect of culture on physical activity behaviors
- To read current literature on pedometers
- To encourage critical thinking

Equipment and Setting

To complete this assignment, students need a copy of the research article "Physical Activity in an Old Order Amish Community" (Bassett, Schneider, & Huntington, 2004). See the reference at the end of this chapter for complete information on the journal in which this article appears.

General Instructions

1. Ask students to read the article by a specific date.
2. Assign the content questions presented on page 139. This can be completed in class or outside of class.
3. Facilitate small-group discussions and then hold a discussion with the entire class specifically on the discussion questions presented on page 139.

Wellness Activity

Wellness, the positive component of health, is multidimensional and requires balancing its five dimensions: physical, spiritual, emotional, social, and intellectual. Achieving wellness means maximizing your potential while taking into account your unique capabilities, heredity, and the environment in which you are surrounded. Although the focus of this book has been on physical activity, physical wellness reciprocally interacts with all the other dimensions of wellness. It is important for students to explore the other realms of wellness and participate in activities that can enhance these areas and improve their overall sense of happiness, productivity, and energy.

Expected Outcomes

- To teach the concept of wellness and its five dimensions: physical, social, spiritual, emotional, and intellectual

Physical Activity and Culture

Students should be able to answer the following questions after reading the pedometer article "Physical Activity in an Old Order Amish Community" by Bassett, Schneider, and Huntington, 2004.

Content Questions

1. In your own words, describe the purpose of this study.
2. What led the researchers to determine the need for such a study?
3. What was the most important factor about the life of the Amish population that instigated the need for investigation?
4. How long did the Amish wear pedometers?
5. Did they have to do anything else besides wear the pedometer and record their step counts?
6. What is a MET?
7. What did the researchers do if they were missing step-count data from participants?
8. Were there gender differences in step counts? If so, what were they and why did they exist?
9. Do you think there would be gender differences in step counts among "typical" Western workers today? Do you think there are "typical" gender patterns of behavior?
10. Were there differences in step counts on particular days of the week? Why or why not?
11. What was the highest one-day total step count for an Amish man and an Amish woman, and why were those daily step counts so high?
12. Did step counts per day decrease with age in this study? How does this compare to previous studies?
13. Discuss the limitations explained by the researchers. Can you think of more limitations? What would have strengthened this study?
14. How do the results apply to the U.S. Surgeon General's recommendation on physical activity and health?

Discussion Questions

1. Why do you think you were given this study to read and discuss?
2. Describe and discuss lifestyles, wellness dimensions, and health indices of the Amish that were different from non-Amish populations. (In this discussion, include factors related to obesity other than physical activity.)

From Robert P. Pangrazi, Aaron Beighle, and Cara L. Sidman, 2007, *Pedometer Power, Second Edition*, (Champaign, IL: Human Kinetics).

- To participate in new activities in each dimension of wellness
- To increase awareness of various behaviors that can improve overall wellness

Equipment and Setting

- Make pedometers available in case students choose an activity that requires a step count.
- Because there are five different activities to complete, students need several days to complete this activity.

General Instructions

1. See pages 141-142 for instructions on how to perform this wellness activity.
2. Have students discuss, both in small groups and as a class, their reaction to completing this assignment in order to facilitate thinking about the concept of wellness and its interacting dimensions.

Final Thoughts

At the secondary and college levels, pedometer activities can be more challenging in order to promote critical thinking skills and healthy lifestyle behaviors. Reading pedometer research and increasing awareness regarding physical activity and step counts give students an opportunity to apply the information in a way that is most meaningful to them.

If You Want to Know More . . .

The following Web sites provide resources for secondary- and college-level physical education teachers and offer supplemental information to enhance teaching and improve curricula.

Web Sites

www.sph.uth.tmc.edu/catch/

The CATCH Web site provides information to help educators, administrators, and parents promote and maintain heart-healthy behaviors in children and adolescents. CATCH, in its long form, is known as the Coordinated Approach to Child Health (formerly, the Child and Adolescent Trial for Cardiovascular Health).

Wellness Activity

Select one activity from each of the five wellness dimensions to complete this semester. Each activity you choose must be something you have never done before. You may perform an activity not listed, but you must specify what it is in the space provided. Because the dimensions overlap, be sure that you complete five different activities, one in each of the five dimensions. Immediately after you have completed each activity, write your reaction to the experience. (Please keep responses for each dimension to one page.) In your reaction, you must respond to all of the following:

- Describe the activity.
- What did you learn from the activity?
- How did you feel about trying this new activity?
- Did you succeed in performing the activity?
- Provide an overall evaluation of your level of wellness in that specific dimension.

Place an X next to one activity per dimension.

Physical Dimension

___ 1. Eat two to four fruit servings and three to five vegetable servings in one day.
___ 2. Try one new physical activity and record your step counts.
___ 3. Wear a seat belt while riding in or driving a car.
___ 4. Eat fewer sweets than usual one day.
___ 5. Drink 12 glasses of water in one day.
___ 6. Consume no more than one alcoholic drink for a full week.
___ 7. Get eight hours of sleep.
___ 8. Get a physical (including blood pressure and cholesterol checks) or dental checkup.
___ 9. Other (must specify): _____

Social Dimension

___ 1. When talking to a friend, perform active listening by rephrasing the ideas for clarification.
___ 2. Go out dancing with friends.
___ 3. Exhibit fairness, justice, and concern in dealing with a person or situation.
___ 4. Call a friend or family member that you have not talked to in at least six months.
___ 5. Join a new recreational or university club.
___ 6. Introduce yourself to one new person.
___ 7. Get involved in a campus activity.
___ 8. Go to dinner with friends.
___ 9. Start a weekly group outing with friends, roommates, or classmates.
___ 10. Other (must specify): _____

(continued)

From Robert P. Pangrazi, Aaron Beighle, and Cara L. Sidman, 2007, *Pedometer Power, Second Edition,* (Champaign, IL: Human Kinetics).

Wellness Activity *(continued)*

Spiritual Dimension

___ 1. Perform meditation, deep breathing, or yoga.
___ 2. Participate in an environmental cleanup project.
___ 3. Go for a walk in nature.
___ 4. Write and personally reflect in a journal.
___ 5. Read something spiritual and discuss it with a friend or family member.
___ 6. Share your personal values and beliefs with a friend, colleague, or family member.
___ 7. Attend a church service.
___ 8. Pray.
___ 9. Sit alone and listen to music.
___10. Contribute time or money to a community project.
___11. Other (must specify): _____

Emotional Dimension

___ 1. Make a list of all the things that make you angry, and brainstorm ways to deal with them.
___ 2. Make a list of all the things that cause you stress, and brainstorm ways to deal with them.
___ 3. List five positive things in your life right now.
___ 4. Express your emotions and feelings to someone openly and honestly.
___ 5. Change the way you think about something that has been worrying you.
___ 6. Find a solution to a problem that has been bothering you for a while.
___ 7. For one full day, laugh as much as possible.
___ 8. Write down all your thoughts and feelings about a personal relationship with someone.
___ 9. Discuss an ongoing problem with someone close to you.
___10. Other (must specify): _____

Intellectual Dimension

___ 1. Read the newspaper one day.
___ 2. Learn about something new that is currently not in your area of study.
___ 3. Find a Web site about a topic you are interested in and read about it.
___ 4. Complete an assignment one week before it is due.
___ 5. Ask a grandparent or older person about something they lived through.
___ 6. Learn one new fact about the universe.
___ 7. Attend a lecture on something new.
___ 8. Read a book for pleasure (not for school).
___ 9. Watch a show on the Discovery Channel or History Channel.
___10. Other (must specify): _____

From Robert P. Pangrazi, Aaron Beighle, and Cara L. Sidman, 2007, *Pedometer Power, Second Edition,* (Champaign, IL: Human Kinetics).

www.ops.org/pe/sec.html

This site on secondary physical education from Omaha Public School's Department of Curriculum and Learning provides links to information on a variety of physical activities.

www.pecentral.org/booksmusic/bookstore/books/secondarytexts.html

This site provides a comprehensive list of secondary physical education books.

www.nationalwellness.org

This is the Web site of the National Wellness Institute, whose mission is to serve professionals and organizations that promote optimal health and wellness in individuals and communities.

http://10000steps.org.au

This is the Web site for Australia's 10,000-steps program.

www.statcan.ca/english/edu/index.htm

Statistics Canada's Web site offers learning resources for teachers and students.

www.education.gov.ab.ca/physicaleducationonline/

Alberta Physical Education Online offers lesson plans and approved resources for K-12 teachers.

www.youthsporttrust.org/

Youth Sport Trust, UK, encourages youth sport participation from ages 8 months to 18 years.

References

Bassett, D.R., Schneider, P.L., & Huntington, G.E. (2004). Physical activity in an old order Amish community. *Medicine and Science in Sports and Exercise, 36*(1), 79-85.

Tudor-Locke, C. (2002). Taking steps toward increased physical activity: Using pedometers to measure and motivate. *President's Council on Physical Fitness and Sports Research Digests, 3*(17), 1-8.

Tudor-Locke, C. & Bassett, D.R. (2004). How many steps/day are enough? Preliminary pedometer indices for public health. *Sports Medicine, 34*(1), 1-8.

Tudor-Locke, C., Sisson, S.B., Collova, T., Lee, S.M., & Swan, P.D. (2005). Pedometer-determined step count guidelines for classifying walking intensity in a young ostensibly healthy population. *Canadian Journal of Applied Physiology, 30*(6), 666-676.

Activities for Families and Communities

This chapter presents school-, community-, and family-based activities that illustrate how to use pedometers to increase physical activity levels in youth. Social support plays an integral role in successfully changing behaviors and can be particularly influential in a child's decision to be physically active. For this reason, methods for increasing family activity levels have the potential to promote lifestyle activity in students (Brustad 1993, 1996; Kimiecik & Horn 1998; Freedson & Evenson 1991). Figure 7.1 offers basic ideas for increasing family physical activity. Strategies for involving families in the use of pedometers are addressed in this chapter. In addition, the ideas to follow could be used in community-based health promotion programs and to assist in the creation of physically active cultures from a school, home, and community perspective.

- Walk to school.
- Park farther away from the store.
- Do not go to the drive-through window; get out of the car and go inside.
- Schedule regular family walks.
- Walk to the store if and when possible.
- Take the stairs instead of the elevator.
- Find innovative ways to make all chores more active.

- Join a YMCA or community center and expose the family to a variety of activities.
- Take dance lessons as a family.
- Limit computer, TV, and inactive time to less than two hours a day.
- Play active outdoor games (weather permitting).
- Wear pedometers and keep step logs.

Figure 7.1   General ways to increase family activity.

Physical Education Nights

Physical education nights offer teachers an excellent opportunity to showcase what they teach in a high-quality physical education program (Morgan & Morgan 2004). They also help establish a physically active culture at the school. Physical education nights can be conducted in two ways: 1) parents observe their children participating in physical education activities, or 2) parents and children participate in physical education activities together. Regardless of the approach, when pedometers are used, physical education nights offer an excellent opportunity to educate families on pedometer use.

Expected Outcomes

- To expose parents to high-quality physical education
- To teach parents they can use pedometers to promote physical activity in their family
- To teach parents about the importance of family activity

Equipment and Setting

- Promotional flier (see figure 7.2)
- One pedometer per family
- Equipment for physical education activities

General Instructions

1. Develop a flier to promote the event. Depending on the size of the school, it might be best to have physical education nights for one grade at a time.
2. Create an agenda, or lesson plan, for the evening. The lesson plan should include a variety of activities. Introduce pedometers early in the lesson, and then refer to them throughout. Activities in chapter 5 are excellent activities to teach during a physical education night. Try to include activities that students can participate in at home.
3. The flow of the evening will depend on the number of participants. If possible, it is best if all parents and children are active together. However, if there are too many participants, it may be necessary for children and parents from specific classes to rotate into the activities.
4. At the conclusion of the program, encourage parents to be active with their children and to discuss physical education activities at home.

Active Open House

Most schools hold an open house sometime during the year. These events offer an excellent chance to educate parents about pedometers and increase awareness of what is being taught in physical education.

Expected Outcomes

- To expose families to pedometers
- To allow parents to wear a pedometer during open house

Performing Tonight

	Activity	Grade level	Activity	Grade level
Introductory activities (warm-up)	New leader	3rd	European running	5th
	Countdown	K	Bend, stretch, and shake	1st
Fitness routines (exercise routines)	Exercises to music	6th	Exercises to music	5th
	Animal walks and fitness challenges	2nd	Astronaut drills	4th
Lesson focus (skills)	Hula hoops	3rd	Juggling	6th
	Skills with balloons	K	Basketball skills	4th
	Tinikling	5th	Tinikling	5th
Games (closing activities)	Odd and even	3rd	Box ball	4th
	Musical ball passing	1st	Musical ball passing	2nd

Figure 7.2 Sample promotional flyer.

Equipment and Setting

- Pedometers to check out
- Tracking sheet to keep track of checked-out pedometers
- Pedometer information sheet

General Instructions

1. Set up a table at the front entrance of the school or the location where most families will enter.
2. As families enter, invite them to check out a pedometer to wear during the open house. If pedometers have already been used during physical education, most children will be excited to have their parents wear the pedometer.
3. Once the pedometer is checked out and the appropriate placement found, have parents participate in the open house as they normally would.
4. Before leaving, ask parents to return the pedometer. This is an excellent time to hand out a physical education newsletter or other fliers promoting physical education events for the year.

Teaching Hints

Some schools include physical education activities as a part of the open house in the form of mini-PE nights, with short activities that begin every five minutes. This allows families to stop in, participate, and then move on to other open house activities. Stations also work well during open houses.

Physical Activity Festival

The school festival is often the highlight of the year for students. With that in mind, why not include physical activities in the festival and make the Physical Activity Festival a lasting memory for students? One approach to these festivals is to create a field day–type atmosphere. Using pedometers to monitor physical activity provides another element of fun to an already fun-filled day.

Expected Outcomes

- To provide families with a safe, fun environment in which to be physically active
- To allow parents and families to wear pedometers and monitor their physical activity level
- To teach families fun activities they can do at home

Equipment and Setting

- Pedometers to be checked out
- Equipment necessary for booths and stations
- Volunteers to work the booths
- School field or other large space

General Instructions

1. Organize a committee to assist in the planning of the event.
2. Establish the booths to be offered and determine the equipment needed. It is important that all of the booths be activity based.
3. Determine the structure of the festival. Will students have to pay for tickets to participate in an activity? Is the festival free of charge and funded by a PTA? Will food and snacks be available?
4. Promote the festival with fliers, morning announcements, advertisements in school papers, and so on.
5. As the event approaches, prepare by collecting necessary equipment in one location, confirm volunteers and times, map out the festival and booths, and take care of other small details.
6. On the day of the event, arrive early to set up the stations and prepare the festival.
7. At the entrance to the festival, set up a booth to check out pedometers. Families can check out pedometers to wear for the duration of the festival. It may even be possible to give a prize for the greatest number of steps taken. You could establish a category for parents and each grade level and award prizes. If pedometers with the physical activity time function are available, you could also give a prize for most minutes and most steps per minute.

Pass the Pedometer

Families can use this activity when walking the dog, participating in a charity walk, or any other family event that involves physical activity.

Expected Outcomes

- To promote family activity
- To increase family members' awareness of their activity levels

General Instructions

1. Every 5 to 10 minutes, the person wearing the pedometer looks at the step count and then passes it to another family member. Other family members guess how many steps were taken.

2. The next family member wears the pedometer for 5 to 10 minutes and the process continues. Each time, the family guesses either the total steps accumulated by everyone (don't reset the pedometer) or the steps accumulated by the last person who wore the pedometer (reset the pedometer at each change).

3. During or after the outing, the family can celebrate their total step counts and discuss why the number of steps may be different for different family members (e.g., stride length). When parents discuss physical activity, they show their children that they value and support physical activity.

Pedometer Chore Time

Wearing a pedometer so you can monitor steps while doing chores is another way to measure the amount of activity accumulated during lifestyle activity. It can increase awareness as to what types of chores result in the greatest number of steps. This information can be valuable for future decisions in trying to accumulate more activity on any given day.

Expected Outcomes

- To allow family members to monitor their physical activity levels while participating in chores

- To increase awareness of the activity involved in lifestyle activities

- To add a sense of excitement to the sometimes tedious chore time

General Instructions

1. Family members make a chart of family chores and include a space to record steps taken while doing the chores. See the Family Chores Step Log on page 152.

2. Family members wear a pedometer while doing their chores.

3. Family members record on a chart the number of steps taken while completing the chore. This chart can be kept on the refrigerator and used for future reference. For example, a child may want to accumulate 300 more steps for the day but has to do a chore of his or her choice. The chart can help the child make an appropriate choice to meet his or her goal.

4. After all chores are finished, the family meets and discusses which chores are active and which are inactive. Also, they can brainstorm and create ways to increase the number of steps taken during relatively inactive chores.

Family Chores Step Log

Chore	Mom	Dad	Child	Child	Average chore step count
Sweeping					
Dusting					
Raking					
Washing windows					
Doing laundry					
Mowing the grass					
Individual total					

From Robert P. Pangrazi, Aaron Beighle, and Cara L. Sidman, 2007, *Pedometer Power, Second Edition,* (Champaign, IL: Human Kinetics).

Errands With a Pedometer

Often families feel they are too busy to exercise because they are constantly running errands. Pedometers allow parents and children to see how much activity they can accumulate while completing errands. In a day of running to the grocery store, going to the mall, and driving to a soccer game, families can accumulate many steps.

Expected Outcomes

- To allow families to track the amount of activity they accumulate while running errands

- To provide families with the information necessary to make lifestyle changes to increase daily physical activity

General Instructions

1. Family members wear a pedometer for several days while running errands.

2. Family members then record the total number of steps taken as well as the number of steps taken for each errand.

3. Calculations of the average number of steps taken by family members while running errands are completed.

4. The family should discuss why one errand may have been more active than another. For example, driving to and watching a soccer game may not produce as many steps as a couple of hours walking at the mall.

5. The family can also discuss how they could change the low-activity days or errands to increase physical activity. For example, park at the far end of the parking lot or take the stairs instead of the elevator or escalator.

Evaluating Physical Activities

Many favorite activities can be put to the test by the use of a pedometer. This test allows both parents and children to measure the number of steps accumulated during their favorite activities (see figure 7.1 on page 146 for some activity ideas).

Expected Outcomes

- To count the steps accumulated during a variety of activities

- To promote family activity

General Instructions

1. Each family member picks an activity for family participation. To evaluate the activity level, family members record the steps they take during that activity.

2. The family keeps a chart of the activities they participate in and the corresponding steps for that activity. The list should be displayed on the refrigerator or in another prominent place in the home.

3. After each test, the family should discuss the level of the day's activity.

4. All family members can seek new and enjoyable activities to test.

Family Goals

Working together toward a common physical activity goal is a way for a family to promote lifestyle activity. It also shows children that activity is valued and supported in a household.

Expected Outcomes

- To develop several activities that all family members can enjoy together
- To work together toward a common physical activity goal

General Instructions

1. Create a log sheet (see page 152 for an example).

2. Each family member wears the pedometer for one day.

3. After every family member has worn the pedometer for one day, they calculate their total number of steps.

4. The family sets a family goal based on this number. A 10 percent increase in total steps is a good start.

5. The family repeats steps 2 and 3.

6. If the family owns or has access to one or two pedometers, each family member can wear the pedometer for four days. Weekend days are useful for showing how activity levels vary when family members are not working or going to school.

Family Dance Night

Because dancing is an enjoyable form of physical activity in which all family members can participate, a regular family dance night can be planned to increase step counts. This activity can be adapted to accommodate specific age levels and numbers of family members.

Expected Outcomes

- To increase family activity by dancing to a variety of music
- To develop and refine basic rhythmic movements in the nonthreatening family environment
- To enhance enjoyment of physical activity

General Instructions

1. Each family member chooses a song he or she wants to dance to during Family Dance Night.
2. Each family member has a number, and one family member randomly selects the order of songs by the numbers. Each week, a different family member chooses the order.
3. Family Dance Night can consist of anything from a formal dance lesson taught by one of the children, as learned in physical education class, to an informal session in which everyone does his or her own thing to the preselected music.
4. The family should record pedometer step counts before and after the dance.

Walk and Talk

Being able to talk with a friend while doing physical activity increases the motivation for many students. Walking and talking is a good way for parents and children to learn about each other without undue interference and distractions.

Expected Outcomes

- To increase physical activity among family members
- To increase communication among family members

General Instructions

1. Family members pair up to take walks on specified days or evenings. Families post a rotating list on the refrigerator, and every effort should be made to ensure that all family members have an opportunity to walk with each other at least once a week.

2. The family should develop a regular rotation for wearing pedometers, depending on the number of pedometers available. For example, if the family has one pedometer, both individuals in a walking pair should have a chance to record their step counts on separate nights.

3. The walk should last at least 10 minutes, and each person should actively participate in a discussion (e.g., about their day, what's on their mind, how to increase their step counts).

4. One night a week, the entire family should walk and talk together.

5. The family should record pedometer step counts on a regular basis.

Walk Around the Clock

All people have different times during the day when they are most active or inactive. A reasonable goal is to try to be active at regular intervals throughout the day. This activity will help create awareness of activity patterns for youth and their parents.

Expected Outcomes

- To increase awareness of physical activity levels throughout the day
- To ultimately increase step counts

General Instructions

1. See page 157 for a sample chart to record step counts around the clock. Note the blanks provided to calculate total step counts during different segments of the day.

2. Family members can be labeled "morning steppers," "afternoon steppers," or "evening steppers" based on which part of the day they accumulate the greatest number of steps.

3. To increase step counts, the family should note which time of the day is the most inactive for each family member and discuss what can be done to make each family member more active during those times, if possible.

Walk Around the Clock

Record your steps each hour, then add up the morning, afternoon, and evening step totals as well as the grand total.

Step Record

A.M.		P.M.	
5:00-6:00	_____	12:00-1:00	_____
6:00-7:00	_____	1:00-2:00	_____
7:00-8:00	_____	2:00-3:00	_____
8:00-9:00	_____	3:00-4:00	_____
9:00-10:00	_____	4:00-5:00	_____
10:00-11:00	_____	5:00-6:00	_____
11:00-12:00 p.m.	_____	6:00-7:00	_____
		7:00-8:00	_____
		8:00-9:00	_____

Morning steps: (5:00 a.m.-12:00 p.m.)

Afternoon steps: (12:00 p.m.-5:00 p.m.)

Evening steps: (5:00 p.m.-9:00 p.m.)

Grand total step count:

From Robert P. Pangrazi, Aaron Beighle, and Cara L. Sidman, 2007, *Pedometer Power, Second Edition,* (Champaign, IL: Human Kinetics).

Family Scavenger Hunt

This enjoyable activity is informal and easy to implement with families. Scavenger hunt items can be found around the house or around the neighborhood if more activity is desired.

Expected Outcomes

- To increase activity levels of family members
- To promote teamwork and cooperation among family members (or neighborhoods)
- To become educated about various topics related to health, wellness, and the environment

General Instructions

1. The family should select scavenger hunt teams of two or more.
2. Each team must have at least one pedometer.
3. See figure 7.3 for scavenger hunt items organized by category. The family should select as many items as necessary to suit their (or their neighborhood's) needs. Gathering the items should promote physical activity as much as possible.
4. The team that returns with the most items and the highest step count is the winner.

Season Stepping

It is easy for the change in seasons to cause a change in the activity levels of children and adults. Learning to be active year-round is important in maintaining a healthy lifestyle.

Expected Outcomes

- To enhance awareness of various obstacles to being physically active year-round
- To become more physically active during less active times of the year

General Instructions

See figure 7.4 on page 160 for ideas for increasing physical activity levels throughout the year as a family. Walking is one activity that can be done in any season.

Choose four items from each category for the first hunt. Each team has a total of $1.00 to complete the scavenger hunt.

Food

1 red apple

1 green apple

1 orange

1 banana

4 purple grapes

1 leaf of lettuce

1 carrot

1 cup of ice cubes

Tools

1 wrench

5 pencils

1 dust pan with brush

1 wooden spoon

Health-Related Items

2 bandages

5 cotton swabs

1 sneaker

1 tennis racket

2 boxing gloves

1 blue ball

Clothing

1 baseball cap

1 pair of blue denim jeans

1 pair of basketball shorts

1 scarf

Figure 7.3   Scavenger hunt items.

Active Samaritans

Teaching students to become productive members of society is important and is a part of developing overall wellness. What better way to do this than to encourage them to be active in community services? In fact, many schools have community service clubs that volunteer for a variety of community service activities in their area. The following is a list of community service projects that incorporate the use of pedometers into school activities.

1. Collect trash on the playground.
2. Rake leaves on school property.
3. Rake leaves in the neighborhood on a Saturday and collect donations for a charity of the students' choice.
4. Participate in a local walkathon for the students' charity of choice in which donations are given per step.
5. Participate in Jump Rope for Heart or Hoops for Heart and collect donations based on the number of jumps or steps.

Fall

Walking to school*
Hiking with family*
Square dancing*
Raking leaves*
Trick-or-treating on Halloween

Winter

Mall walking*
Shoveling snow
Building a snowman
Snowshoeing
Christmas caroling
Carrying wood into the house*

Spring

Gardening
Fun walk or run*
Nature walks*
Lawn mowing*
Walking to the local store*

Summer

Walking on the beach
Visiting an amusement park*
Visiting a zoo*
Visiting a local park*
Neighborhood walk to clean up trash*
Playing outdoor games* (e.g., tag, hopscotch, jump rope, modified ball games to promote success)

* Activities that can be performed in more than one season.

Figure 7.4   Seasonal stepping ideas for the family.

Adopt-a-Neighborhood Street

Adopting a portion of a highway to keep free of litter is a common civic activity throughout the United States. On a local basis, it is an excellent activity for children and parents as they work together to keep neighborhood streets clean.

Expected Outcomes

- To increase activity levels of family members
- To develop family unity
- To help the environment

General Instructions

1. Parents should adopt a neighborhood street in their area, and the whole family should participate. Be sure to wear gloves and bring plastic bags.

2. The family should wear pedometers and record step counts after each street-cleanup outing.

Behavior-Change Contract

As discussed in chapter 4, it is important to develop and practice self-management skills in order to facilitate behavior changes that last a lifetime. Making a behavior-change contract either as an individual, as a class, as a family, or as a community group is one way to work on these skills, which can aid in increasing physical activity. Using step-count goals after attaining a baseline step count can be incorporated into any behavior-change contract. See pages 162-164 for a sample contract.

Walk-to-School Day

Active commuting to school is an important opportunity for children to accumulate greater physical activity. International, national, and local programs exist to encourage walking or bicycling to school to promote health, protect the environment, and rally for safer streets. The section If You Want to Know More . . . lists Web sites with ideas on how to get

Walking to school instead of driving gets both parents and children moving.

Behavior-Change Contract

Follow the steps below to create a contract to increase your physical activity and make changes in behavior that will last a lifetime.

Step 1: Record your daily step counts for seven days and complete the Baseline Step Log. (This contract may be modified to meet your individual or group needs.)

Baseline Step Log

Instructions:

1. Press the reset button every morning.
2. Secure the pedometer to your waistband in a vertical position with the lid closed. The pedometer will not accurately measure your steps if you attach it to a loose waistband.
3. Secure the safety strap to your clothes to prevent loss and limit damage.
4. Do not increase your physical activity just because you are wearing the pedometer. Keep your routine as normal as possible.
5. Record your step counts every day for a week.
6. If you forget to wear the pedometer one day, write "forgot" in the comments section. For full credit you must complete at least four weekdays and one weekend day.

Day	Date	Total # of daily steps	Total # of times you opened the pedometer*	Check here if you performed any activity out of the ordinary	Comments (If you did extra activity, describe it here.)
1					
2					
3					
4					
5					
6					
7					
Weekly total # of steps					
Average daily step count					

* If you can't remember exactly how many times you opened the pedometer, give your best estimate.

From Robert P. Pangrazi, Aaron Beighle, and Cara L. Sidman, 2007, *Pedometer Power, Second Edition*, (Champaign, IL: Human Kinetics).

Write additional comments about your week: _____

_____

_____

Step 2: Read and sign the following behavior-change contract. Have a witness sign it to hold you accountable for your decision to change. (This contract may be modified to establish goals for a group.)

I, _____, agree to the following goals in
(print name)

order to improve my health and wellness and achieve a successful behavior change by _____.
(print date)

My baseline step count is _____.

I will increase my step count by _____ steps per day until I reach my final step-count goal of _____ steps per day.

I will change the following behaviors in order to increase my step counts (fill out all that apply):

❏ I will walk to school at least ____ days per week.

❏ I will play outside with my friends at least ____ days per week.

❏ I will reduce my use of TV, electronic games, and computers to only _____ minutes per day.

❏ Other: _____

Signature: _____ Date: _____

Witness signature: _____ Date: _____

Step 3: After a minimum of four weeks engaging in more physical activity and recording your step counts, complete the Final Step Log and answer the final reaction questions to help you determine the success of this activity.

Final Step Log

Instructions:

1. Press the reset button every morning.

2. Secure the pedometer to your waistband in a vertical position with the lid closed. The pedometer will not accurately measure your steps if you attach it to a loose waistband.

3. Secure the safety strap to your clothes to prevent loss and limit damage.

(continued)

From Robert P. Pangrazi, Aaron Beighle, and Cara L. Sidman, 2007, *Pedometer Power, Second Edition,* (Champaign, IL: Human Kinetics).

Behavior-Change Contract *(continued)*

4. Do not increase your physical activity just because you are wearing the pedometer. Keep your routine as normal as possible.

5. Record your step counts every day for a week.

6. If you forget to wear the pedometer one day, just write "forgot" in the comments section. For full credit you must complete at least four weekdays and one weekend day.

Day	Date	Total # of steps	Total # of times you opened the pedometer*	Check here if you performed any activity out of the ordinary	Comments (If you did extra activity, describe it here.)
1					
2					
3					
4					
5					
6					
7					
Total # of steps					
Average daily step count					

* If you can't remember exactly how many times you opened the pedometer, give your best estimate.

Final Reaction

Answer the following questions in complete sentences. Use correct spelling and proper grammar.

1. Compare and contrast your final step log with your baseline step log. Were there similarities and differences? Did your step counts increase, decrease, or stay the same? Explain why.

2. Did you reach the goals you outlined in your behavior-change contract? Why or why not?

3. Did you learn anything by wearing the pedometer? If so, what? If not, why not?

4. Do you plan to continue to wear the pedometer? If yes, in what capacity? If no, why not?

From Robert P. Pangrazi, Aaron Beighle, and Cara L. Sidman, 2007, *Pedometer Power, Second Edition*, (Champaign, IL: Human Kinetics).

involved. You can easily incorporate pedometers into these events by using them to monitor step counts and analyzing the difference after adding an active walk to and from school. School, group, and individual goals can be set to encourage greater participation and motivation for continued active commuting.

Other Pedometer Activity Ideas

There is no limit to the school-, community-, and family-based activities you can develop using pedometers to increase physical activity and promote active cultures. For example, having students organize and develop a stepathon is a great way to raise funds, promote physical activity, and facilitate a sense of community. The stepathon can also help enhance the multiple dimensions of wellness: physical, emotional, spiritual, intellectual, and social. In addition, designating one day as Step It Up Day, where students actively engage in as much lifestyle, recreational, and leisure activity as possible, can be a way to get people talking and excited about being active.

Lastly, having students or family members create physically active cultures by posting signs as prompts for physical activity can foster creativity and improvement of the school, community, and home environment. Researchers have demonstrated that posting a simple sign at the point of decision to take the stairs instead of the escalator can increase physical activity (Brownwell, Stunkard, & Albaum, 1980). A message as simple as "Be healthy, take the stairs," may make a difference in the number of steps accumulated throughout the course of a day. Different groups can come together and create these signs to post throughout the school, community, and even your home to remind people that even small steps count. The Web site www.smallstep.gov, sponsored by the U.S. government, provides information and resources on ways to incorporate small changes into the lifestyles of adults, teens, and kids.

Final Thoughts

Combating the childhood obesity epidemic is a complex challenge, but one that deserves constant attention, valuable resources, and a steadfast commitment. Because of our predominately fast-paced, technologically-driven, sedentary culture, going out of our way to support and promote physically active environments is crucial, not only from school-based, but from family-based and community-based approaches as well. Physical educators, school administrators, legislators, policy makers, parents, and family members owe it to our youth, who may be facing a lifetime of chronic disease and other debilitating conditions, to find ways to support and facilitate healthy behaviors in order to achieve the quality of life, optimal functioning, and high level of wellness they so richly deserve.

If You Want to Know More . . .

The following Web sites offer information about promoting physical activity in different ways that families can enjoy together.

Web Sites

www.valinet.com/~dbotkin

Daniel Botkin (professional footbagger, social worker, and coach) has put together an informative Web site that focuses on teaching and mentoring marginalized youth using sports, crafts, and peer education.

www.lensaunders.com/aces/aces.html

This Web site provides information about Project ACES (All Children Exercise Simultaneously), which takes place annually (usually in May because it's National Physical Fitness and Sports Month). On the designated day, school children either exercise, walk, jog, bike, dance, do aerobics, or a combination of any of these activities for 15 to 45 minutes.

www.ymca.net

The Web site of the YMCA of the USA provides links to local YMCAs.

www.americanheart.org/presenter.jhtml?identifier=2281

The Web site of American Heart Walk is sponsored by the American Heart Association.

www.americanheart.org/presenter.jhtml?identifier=2360

This Web site provides information about Jump Rope for Heart, an educational fund-raising event that teaches students the benefits of physical activity, how to keep their hearts healthy, and how they can help save lives in their own community.

www.beactivenc.org

This Web site provides information about how this organization encourages North Carolinians to create the policies, opportunities, facilities, and motivation to promote physical activity and good health. Participants in the Be Active steps program can log the number of steps they take (counted by a pedometer) daily on the Web site, and kids can take fun quizzes.

www.dot.ca.gov/hq/maint/adopt/coordinators.htm

This Web site provides information about California's Adopt-a-Highway program.

www.walktoschool.org

This Web site provides information about International Walk to School events and promotes safe walking and bicycling to school throughout the year.

www.iwalktoschool.org

This is the official Web site of International Walk to School. The goal of the walk varies from community to community. Some walks rally for safer and improved streets, some to promote healthier habits, and some to protect the environment. Whatever the reason, International Walk to School events encourage a more walkable world—one community at a time.

www.saferoutesinfo.org

Safe Routes to School programs all share the goal of improving the health of kids and the community by making walking and bicycling to school safer, easier, and more enjoyable.

www.smallstep.gov

This Web site provides a list of small steps to help adults, teens, and kids become active and eat better. It is an excellent resource for ideas that make a difference.

www.travelsmart.gov.au/schools/schools2.html

This Web site provides information on Australia's Walking School Bus programs.

www.phac-aspc.gc.ca/guide/index_e.html

This Web site provides Canada's guide to healthy living and physical activity.

www.ymca.ca

YMCA Canada provides activities and programs for people of all ages.

www.goforgreen.ca

This Web site provides information about Go for Green, Active Living and Environmental Solutions.

www.livingschool.ca

This Web site is for an OPHEA initiative promoting healthy, active, open school communities.

www.walkingbus.com/index.htm

This Web site describes a UK walking bus scheme in action.

www.whi.org.uk

This UK Web site provides information and advice about Walking the Way to Health.

References

Brownwell, K.D., Stunkard, A.J., & Albaum, J.M. (1980). Evaluation and modification of exercise patterns in the natural environment. *American Journal of Psychiatry, 137,* 1540-1545.

Brustad, R.J. (1993). Who will go out and play? Parental and psychological influences on children's attraction to physical activity. *Pediatric Exercise Science, 5,* 210-223.

Brustad, R.J. (1996). Attraction to physical activity in urban schoolchildren: Parental socialization and gender influences. *Research Quarterly for Exercise and Sport, 67,* 316-323.

Freedson, P.S., & Evenson, S. (1991). Familial aggregation in physical activity. *Research Quarterly for Exercise and Sport, 62,* 384-389.

Kimiecik, J.C., & Horn, T.S. (1998). Parental beliefs and children's moderate-to-vigorous physical activity. *Research Quarterly for Exercise and Sport, 69,* 163-175.

Morgan, C.L., & Morgan, C.F. (2004). Promoting physical activity: Physical Education Nights. *Teaching Elementary Physical Education, 15*(5), 33-35.

About the Authors

Robert P. Pangrazi, PhD, is a respected physical education professor, researcher, and author. He has written 51 textbooks and more than 100 research and journal articles related to youth fitness and physical education. Dr. Pangrazi has been a keynote speaker for 29 state and district conventions and an invited speaker at nearly 200 conferences. He has presented in Canada, Sweden, Britain, Australia, and the Czech Republic. Dr. Pangrazi is a fellow of the American Academy of Kinesiology and Physical Education, an elected position limited to 125 members nationally. He also

is an honor fellow in the American Alliance for Health, Physical Education, Recreation and Dance.

Dr. Pangrazi lives in Tempe, Arizona, and serves as a consultant for Walk4Life and Gopher Sport. He is a professor emeritus at Arizona State University and was a classroom teacher and physical education specialist. In his free time, Dr. Pangrazi enjoys walking, mountain biking, hiking, playing the guitar, and reading.

An assistant professor in the department of kinesiology and health promotion at the University of Kentucky, **Aaron Beighle, PhD,** has extensive experience conducting pedometer research with children and working with teachers who use pedometers in schools. Many of these pursuits have resulted in published research and applied professional articles. A member of the American Alliance for Health, Physical Education, Recreation and Dance (AAHPERD), the National Association for Sport and Physical Education (NASPE), and the National Association for Kinesiology and

Physical Education in Higher Education (NAKPEHE), he has presented at the local, state, regional, and national level. Aaron enjoys spending time with his wife, Barbara, and daughter, Faith, as well as traveling and

participating in a variety of physical activities. He resides in Lexington, Kentucky.

Cara L. Sidman holds a PhD in exercise and wellness, for which she prepared a dissertation and subsequent publications regarding the use of pedometers in promoting and adhering to physical activity. In addition, she has presented at regional and national conferences on topics related to behavior change, environmental influences on behavior, lifetime fitness and wellness, and physical activity adherence among sedentary women. A member of AAHPERD and the National Association for Kinesiol-

ogy and Physical Education in Higher Education (NAKPEHE), Cara is an assistant professor in the department of health, physical education, recreation, and coaching at the University of Wisconsin at Whitewater. She has developed an interest and expertise in the use of technology in teaching and learning and continues to focus her scholarly efforts on university and community populations. In her leisure time, she enjoys reading, jogging, dancing, and enhancing her wellness.

*You'll find
other outstanding
physical activity resources at*

www.HumanKinetics.com

In the U.S. call

1-800-747-4457

Australia.............................. 08 8372 0999

Canada 1-800-465-7301

Europe..................... +44 (0) 113 255 5665

New Zealand.................. 0064 9 448 1207

HUMAN KINETICS
The Information Leader in Physical Activity
P.O. Box 5076 • Champaign, IL 61825-5076 USA